"To be a Kenyan and survive, you need to be a Shapeshifter."

THE TRUE STORY OF DAVID MUNYAKEI : GOLDENBERG WHISTLEBLOWER
By Billy Kahora

KWANI? SERIES
is published by Kwani Trust
P.O. Box 2895 00100,
Nairobi, Kenya
Tel: +254 020 232 7294/ 374 5210

E-mail: info@kwani.org

ISBN: 9966-7008-9-7
Cover photography: Amunga Eshuchi
Cover illustration: Black Butterfly Limited
Design and layout: Sokoletu Creative Limited

Kwani Trust
is a Ford Foundation grantee

www.kwani.org

For David Sadera Munyakei.
1968 - 2006

Cast of Characters

Olokurto, Narok

Sadera Munyakei David, farmer, also known as 'Ole Shumpai' (pronounced Ole Shubai) meaning 'white man.' Also known as 'Raju' to his Muslim wife, short for Rajab.
Mariam Sadera, his wife, maiden name Mariam Ali Muhammad Hani
His three daughters aged between 2 and 6: **Naima, Fatma and Sally**
Elizabeth Sembeyo, his mother (deceased)
Daniel Munyakei, his brother
Milka Wambui Munyakei, his grandmother
Emily Munyakei, his aunt

Central Bank of Kenya, Nairobi

David Munyakei, clerk, Development Department, Banking Division
Meshack Onyango Jamasai, Deputy Director
Mr Sisenda, Signatory B, Deputy Departmental Head Development Department
Mr Njoroge, Signatory A, Departmental Head, Development Department, Banking Division,
Mr Kiambati, clerk who trained Munyakei on the job when he joined CBK. (deceased)

Ganjoni and Bamburi, Mombasa

David the fugitive, eventually Rajab after he became a Muslim
Mariam Ali Muhammad Hani, David's wife
Peter Kariuki, best friend and drinking mate
Samuel Njenga, second best friend and drinking mate
Janet, David's girlfriend before he got married

Transparency International

Felgona Atieno, Assistant Programme Officer Communications
Jack Muriuki, Programme Officer, Advocacy and Coalition Building

Chronology of Events

21st June 1968   David Sadera Munyakei is born in Langata Women's Prison, Nairobi.

1974   He is taken to Olokurto, Narok District by his mother, Elizabeth Sembeyo to live with his grandmother, Milka Wambui Munyakei. He starts his education in Olokurto Primary School.

November 1991   Munyakei is employed by the Central Bank after attending Narok High School, Chavakali Secondary School and Knowhow International College in Nairobi.

April 1992   Only months after he's employed and working in the Development Department of the Banking Division, Munyakei starts noticing irregularities in the export compensation claims he has been processing.

April 1992   The Daily Nation publishes a series of stories written by Business Editor Peter Warutere about the ongoing scam. Nothing comes of this.

April 1993	Local banks claim Ksh24 billion from the Central Bank.
April 1993	After approaching Onyango Jamasai, a friend and senior officer , David Munyakei meets Members of Parliament Paul Muite and Peter Anyang' Nyong'o, then in the Opposition, through a former CBK employee, T Kiambati, and hands over evidence of the goings-on at the Central Bank.
April 1993	Prof Anyang' Nyong'o denied permission to table documents in Parliament.
April1993	Sarah Elderkin publishes a series of stories in the Daily Nation that alerts the public to Goldenberg.
May1993	Two days after Elderkin's article is published, Munyakei is arrested at the Central Bank Security Office and taken to Criminal Investigation Department Headquarters at Kilimani. He is transferred to Kileleshwa Police Station and is charged in court a week later with contravening the Official Secrets Act. He is denied bail and taken to Industrial Area Remand Prison.
June-July 1993	Elizabeth Sembeyo visits her son at the Industrial Area Remand

and immediately goes into combined depression and high blood pressure. Two days later, she suffers a stroke and goes into a coma.

July 10, 1993   Elizabeth Sembeyo passes away while still comatose.

July 1993   Munyakei goes to court for a mention of his case and is granted a bond of Kshs 200,000. He is asked to report to Court and the CBK while the Attorney-General reviews his case.

September 1993   The A-G enters a nolle prosequi declaring there is no case against David Sadera Munyakei and after months of hardship he is finally a free man.

September 1993   In spite of his innocence, the Central Bank of Kenya declare they no longer have confidence in Munyakei and send him a letter of immediate dismissal.

November 1993   Munyakei applies for his job back at the CBK, to no avail.

Late 1994   After almost a year of living in Ongata Rongai, Munyakei flees to Mombasa after being warned by friends that his life is in danger after escalation of Goldenberg exposés. He carries documents, as evidence of the fraudulent goings-on at CBK.

1994	He starts working for Standard Newspapers as an advertising executive but leaves after a year.
1995	He joins Nation Newspapers in the same position.
1997	Munyakei converts to Islam and later marries Mariam Ali Muhammad Hani after a year-long courtship. He also starts working as a sales manager for a furniture company.
Early 1998	David's first daughter, Naima Munyakei, is born.
Mid 1998	Munyakei leaves the furniture company and joins the ranks of the unemployed.
Late 1998	Munyakei leaves Mombasa and travels to Olokurto in Narok with his wife and child where he begins leading a peaceful rural existence that is uninterrupted for 4 years.
2002	Narc government is elected and declares its commitment to fight corruption.
Early 2003	Justice Minister Kiraitu Murungi reopens the Goldenberg issue.
March 14, 2003	The Goldenberg Commission starts

12

its work.

Late 2003   Munyakei voluntarily travels to Nairobi and introduces himself to Joseph Kamau, now chief of CID, offering to testify at Goldenberg. He also travels to Mombasa to retrieve the Goldenberg documents he had hidden there years earlier.

December 2003   David Sadera Munyakei testifies at the Goldenberg Commission. Lawyer, Gatonye Waweru says that if there were just 10 witnesses like Munyakei, the Commission's work would be done. John Khaminwa is so impressed that he asks Munyakei to have a cup of tea with him so they can have a chat.

September 2004   Transparency International visits David Munyakei in Olokurto.

October 2004   The Nation publishes a story on David Munyakei.

October 2004   Munyakei wins the Integrity Award. Justice Minister Kiraitu Murungi orders David Munyakei to report back to work with PS John Githongo and others present during the Integrity Awards ceremony. Nothing comes of this.

November 2004 The Standard publishes an in-depth

piece on David Munyakei.

January 2005	Munyakei is offered a job at the Office of the President at a net monthly salary of KSh 8000 a month. He declines.
February 2005	Munyakei wins the Firimbi award presented by the Kenya National Commission on Human Rights.
January 2006,	Munyakei is forced by circumstances to accept the job at the Office of the President at a salary of 8,000.
June 2006	Munyakei falls ill in Narok
July 31st 2006	Munyakei dies penniless in a Narok Hospital.

Part 1:
Flight to Mombasa

'Mombasa is like a disco. If you can pay, you are in.'

(Peter Kariuki, Munyakei's best friend in the coastal city, on first meeting him)

EARLY ONE MORNING in December 1993, 6.45, the day's first Nairobi to Mombasa Coast Bus, white with green and yellow stripes, chugged into the Mwembe Tayari bus station. The bus was running late, and the town was already awake, the morning bustle in full swing. Shouts of "Kumanina!" filtered through the bus windows from the crowded station. Vendors were selling kaimatis, kashatas, kahawa tungu and coloured water in small sachets. Many passengers now opened their windows, which had remained shut for most of the journey to keep out the cold inland breezes around Mtito Andei and beyond. But opening the windows did not help; the air was already muggy even at that hour. The effect was sauna-like and the passengers sweated freely. Having left Nairobi at 10 p.m the previous night, they began to feel the pressures of the capital city dissipate.

Cramps uncramped, uncertainty dissolved as the mixed board of old hands and newcomers to this ancient Port wearily stepped out, blinking in the sun's glare. For those not new to Mombasa the heat was a renewal. For the uninitiated, there was a strange sensation – it seemed that their sense of smell had suddenly disappeared. The humidity blocked the nostrils and sinuses and all senses became one in the warm embrace of the heavy air. As the passengers disembarked, the turnboy laughed, 'Hii ndio Mombasa. Karibu!' As he said this he removed his shirt to expose a bony chest.

'Kumanina zenu,' he shouted to no one in particular.

One of the travellers on the Coast Bus was a light-skinned young man of 25 - we'll call him David for now, just as he was to tell all those he would meet during what became his Mombasa years. Call me David. Actually he was more than light-skinned, he was of mixed race - in the casually derogatory Nairobi term, a Point Five or Pointy. In Nairobi, he was always visible, a curiosity; here, in the racial melting pot of Mombasa, his light skin immediately blended in. When David stepped down from the bus onto the soil of Mombasa, he was making a step of faith. He was new to Mombasa and more than most, he must have felt relief at placing his feet on firm ground. He was running away from many things, not least the law, or some perversion of it, for, in the 1990s in Kenya, the law was the president and his cronies. Anybody observing David then would have noted that he was dressed in too many layers of clothes. In hot and humid Mombasa, his overdressed state practically shouted that he wasn't a native, in spite of his skin colour, which marked him as an Arab or a Mswahili or any of the light-skinned peoples that pepper the Kenyan coast. Later, when he began to take on coastal ways, people would take him for a Mbarawa - a coastal community of Somali origin. But unlike any Coast native's, David's skin would soon break out into bright red splotches in the Mombasa sun.

Mombasa in early 1994 was in many ways a great place for a young man trying to make a fresh start. President Moi and the ruling party Kanu had been re-elected two years ago and there was a renewed sense of confidence in the rampant corruption going on everywhere in the country. Like Nairobi, Mombasa was flush with cash from the recent elections - there were deals to be made everywhere. Moi's 'informal economy,' the mainstay of most 'unemployed' Kenyans, meant there was much more cash being exchanged in backstreet alleys and in between containers at the Port than in Mombasa's formal economy. Unlike Nairobi, Mombasa was pleasing to a young man's eye. It was relatively easy to survive, and for someone with David's light skin acceptance was immediate. In Nairobi people mistook him for a mzungu and thought him ripe for a con.

David wore both a jacket and a light sweater and carried a light bag, which contained one solitary pair of trousers and four shirts. It was not that he had left Nairobi in a hurry, having spent almost a year since the misfortunes that had finally caused his flight had befallen him. The light bag was a sign of hard times. By the time he got to Mombasa, he was almost destitute. And the reason he had fled Nairobi was inside his sweater: a package of official bank documents that he kept touching as if to make sure they were still there. In his walk, as he made his way out of the bus station, there was the furtiveness of the fugitive- a hangover from Nairobi. David would eventually convince himself that he had nothing to fear in this place, especially with his light skin – the reason that his friends had recommended he flee to Mombasa. Now he headed towards the Standard Newspapers office on Nkrumah Road, which is on the way to Fort Jesus, next to the ABN Amro Bank.

In his pocket there was a crumpled piece of paper with a name and a phone number, given to him by a friend – a certain Waweru of Standard Newspapers Nairobi. The name on the piece of paper was Mrs. Hatim, the advertising manager at Standard Newspapers Mombasa. She was expecting David.

When David was ushered into her office, Mrs Hatim did not ask him too many questions, even though she had learnt that David had worked for Central Bank and had been sacked. He was looking to make a new start. Told to report for work the next day, he left thinking 'sasa niku survive' – a Nairobi thought if ever there was one, foreign to the laidback culture of Mombasa. The sales representative job, whose grand-sounding official title was 'advertising executive' did not come with a salary. The title had been introduced to differentiate it from the newspaper distribution agents, who were called sales representatives. David would earn a commission on what he sold. To be successful in sales, one needs contacts and a penchant for networking. Difficult even in Nairobi, sales can be a nightmare in smaller towns, and this makes the young salesman in a place like Mombasa prey to temptation. For a young man who knew absolutely no one in Mombasa the new job was a test of what David was made of. He would earn 10 per cent of the value of the advertising space he sold.

David spent his first night in Mombasa at a cheap boarding and lodging downtown. Over the next months he would stay with a high-ranking bank official, a distant relative. During that time, he got to know other advertising executives at the Standard. The reps had been in the game for a while and David soon met Peter Kariuki, a tall, gangly, quick-witted young man with slightly discoloured teeth. Kariuki was 27, only two years older than David. He had been in Mombasa only six months, working in the Circulation Department, but he already came across as an old Pwani hand.

David and Kariuki hit it off immediately and after a month David moved in with his new friend, who lived in a bedsitter in Ganjoni with his brother Ndungu and a friend named Njenga.

'Lazima unifundishe kusurvive,' David told him. You must teach me how to survive.

'Mombasa is like a disco. If you can pay, you are in,' Kariuki laughed.

Around this time, David, who had until now been carrying the documents he had smuggled out of the Central Bank on his person, felt settled enough to seek a more permanent hiding place for them. Later, he would say he buried them in a safe place, but remain evasive about details. Slowly, with the help of fellow exiled Nairobians Kariuki, Ndungu and Njenga, David eased into the life of Mombasa. The first few months were rough. Though Mombasa was flush with cash, the young men went through hard times, especially in those first months. David remembers walking into kiosks so hungry that he would order food without any money in his pocket. Blurting this out after having eaten his fill, he would sit shamefaced and let the inevitable stream of insults wash over him. Such was the difference between Nairobi and Mombasa. In Nairobi, he would have ended up with a beating or in a police cell. These early years were so hard that David would recount details to anyone who would listen. He would remember how his first mattress was a rolled-up wire mesh. Luckily, it was always warm in Mombasa.

Ganjoni is a lower middle-class area of stone houses with makuti roofs. The bed-sitter the four young men lived in was a large room that served as kitchen, bedroom and sitting room, with a small adjoining toilet and bathroom. After a few months, the quartet started experiencing success in fits and starts. They were young and single and so, like moths, they were drawn to the Mombasa bar circuit, frequenting Uncle Sam's, Kigotho's, Sky's and that Mombasa lifestyle staple of the 1990s – Casablanca. They chased clients trying to sell advertising space by day and were in turn chased as clients of a different sort by night in all the watering holes they became recognisable patrons in.

Kariuki describes the young David as well groomed, intelligent, confident and street-smart. He says their friendship in Mombasa was like that of many other young men forced together in a foreign environment - friendship of convenience. Moreover, David made a wonderful drinking and womanising companion. Kariuki did observe some flaws in his new friend, though these were not serious enough to warrant a parting of the ways. David had a sly side to him. He shirked his duties in the house, never cleaning up or cooking when it was his turn. No woman was off-limits to David - including his roommates' girlfriends, at whom he regularly made passes behind their backs.

Many a time, David would borrow small amounts of money that he never repaid. He could also be pushy and demanding, especially with Kariuki's younger brother Ndungu. The earnest, honest young man was becoming an opportunist. There was a power hierarchy in the small Ganjoni house. Kariuki, who owned a car and earned the most, was boss in this company of men. Ndungu, who was largely dependent on his brother, was the youngest and at the bottom of the food chain. David soon made Ndungu his errand boy, his kanda ya moko.

At the time David left Nairobi, he had been living with a Taita girl called Janet in Ongata Rongai, a fast growing township just outside Nairobi. She now began visiting him in Mombasa over weekends, staying in hotels in town or with a cousin in Bamburi. Kariuki describes her as a tall mjuaji (know-it-all) girl from Nairobi. Not far from where Janet's cousin lived was a small kibanda that sold 'vegetables, fruit and other takataka' as its Bajun female vendor would describe it years later. She was then 14 years old and had been born and raised in Lamu - an historical island enclave 200 kilometres north of Mombasa that in the time of the Zanzibari sultans had been forbidden to non-Muslims - by strict Muslim parents. Her name was Mariam Ali Muhammad Hani and she had only recently moved to Mombasa with her older sister, who worked in town. The sister had started the business for her when Mariam had finished her Quran studies in the Madrasa.

Most historical accounts describe the Bajun as a mixture of Bantu, Somali, and Arabs, who maintain themselves as a distinct cultural group. Living primarily in the district of Lamu on the Indian Ocean coast, the Bajun speak a language they call Tikuu, a dialect of Kiswahili. The Bajun evolved when Arab traders began coming to the coast of Kenya to trade and eventually settle. Over the decades, as the Arabs intermarried with the African population, a Muslim community grew. As time passed, the Arabs introduced their social structure to the family-oriented Africans.

It is said that the way of life among the Bajun has changed very little in the past thousand years. Because the Bajun live near the water, most make their living through occupations connected with the sea. They are fishermen, sailors, ocean merchants, shipbuilders, and the like. Some are also engaged in farming. Their main foods are coconut, fish, and rice.

The Bajun community conduct their affairs according the laws of Islam, with a Muslim judge, or kadhi, handling both criminal and civil disputes within the community. The woman's place among the Bajun is in the home, and older Bajun women customarily only leave the house to visit other homes or to go to the market. Mariam's mother, for instance, did her visiting late in the afternoon when the housework was finished and the children were at play. Her father would meanwhile meet with the other men at the mosque or the town square.

Like most Bajun children, Mariam stayed at home until the age of six or seven, and was then sent to the Muslim madrassa where she learnt to read and recite the Koran, say her prayers five times a day, and lead a moral life. The Bajuns' lives revolve around the mosque. In the course of saying five prayers a day, they also wash at least five times. Every Muslim parent ensures that his

24

child receives a basic Islamic education. When a child is born, it is held up by either the father, a friend, or a teacher, who recites the traditional call of prayer into its ear. From the moment of birth, the child is steeped in the lore of Islam. When Mariam met David, she was an open–faced, exuberant girl; she possesses what poets call an 'inner beauty.' Her enthusiasm for life is infectious, and she is as open and honest as the Mombasa day is bright and warm. Mariam says that when she met David, she looked older than her 14 years, having been brought up by five older sisters who had conferred womanly household responsibilities on her since she was 10. She was accustomed to taking care of her sisters' children and even in her early teens was easing into that comfortable indolent physical spread so typical of Swahili women. Mariam, besides selling 'vegetables, fruit and other takataka,' also worked in a nearby saloon and soon became fast friends with David's girlfriend Janet, whose hair she plaited regularly and whose hands and feet she hennaed. Mariam's contact with David was minimal. Now and then he would come over to her stall to buy fruits.

'Habari-yagho! Fungia-mimi-hiyo,' he would say in his strange brusque way. Hello. Wrap up these fruits for me.

Later she would laugh and say: 'The first time I heard that voice, I was taken aback. It was so Baara (inland). So foreign to Mombasa. Nairobi kabisa!' In truth, David's Kiswahili accent must have been almost un-placeably guttural but not wholly pastoral, it was layered with numerous influences from different corners of Kenya. Mariam says his accent stood out all the more because

David tended to speak mostly in English. Despite her limited contact with him, Mariam had a lot of time to observe life on the street where her stall stood, and she would often see the couple pass by holding hands. Though from a strict Muslim family, she had had platonic contact with young men in Lamu (such friendships are not totally frowned upon between young Bajun men and women) and did not find the couple's public displays of affection strange. Though she cannot remember when exactly she stopped seeing them in the neighborhood, Mariam says it was definitely late 1994. Unknown to her, David's relationship with his girlfriend was souring and once Janet stopped coming to Mombasa, David no longer had reason to appear in Bamburi. He reappeared in Mariam's life two years later, as suddenly as he had left, with what seemed to Mariam a highly comical request.

Meanwhile, back in Ganjoni, David had changed jobs from the Standard to the Nation newspapers in 1995. According to David, the latter newspaper was more popular during those years and there was more money to be made by selling advertising in the Nation.

As the months passed and David managed to reinvent himself with a modicum of success, events elsewhere that he had set in motion were moving at breakneck speed. Based on how they knew him, many of David's present friends would have hardly credited him with revealing the scandal that was starting to become a daily feature in the papers by 1996. It had first surfaced in 1993, when Opposition MPs Anyang' Nyong'o and Paul Muite revealed in Parliament what was going on in the Central Bank of Kenya.

At the time, all that existed of the scandal were torrid

debates in Parliament and a series of dry and technical pieces about the scandal written by Nation Business Editor Peter Warutere a whole year earlier. Mostly documentary evidence and business journalese, the pieces had gone largely unnoticed and hardly spelled out the implications of the largest financial pata potea in Africa at the time (pata potea is a rigged street card game popular in Nairobi's downtown back alleys).

Then, recently resigned corruption czar John Githongo, responding to a report in The Independent of London, wrote a prescient passage in his 'Political Diary' column in the July 1993 issue of the Nairobi-based Executive magazine: 'To me, the Goldenberg saga marks a turning point in the development of corruption in Kenya. For the first time in this nation's history, a single set of deals is having macroeconomic implications... it is shaking the very foundations of Kenya's economy... The country has started to consume itself, like the Chinese serpent that is depicted as eating its own tail...' But it was a single article by an elderly white Nation journalist, Sarah Elderkin, a little later, that started the hue and cry. After the article appeared, the IMF and World Bank cried foul and Moi called for investigations to pacify Bretton Woods. Then the weekly Economic Review, now edited by Peter Warutere, got its teeth into the story and refused to let go till Pattni was briefly arrested, for the first time, in March 1994. The Goldenberg circus had begun. Bring in the clowns.

In retrospect, Goldenberg seems to have started the decline of the gilded age of the Moi years. It seems that after the Kanu victory and resurgence in 1992, there was no force capable of challenging Moi and the ruling party.

Then Goldenberg began triggering exposure of scandal after scandal and the hounds started nipping at the old man's heels. Even if it would take another10 years (far short of the 100 years the old man had prophesied KANU would rule) for Moi to finally leave State House and the real story of Goldenberg to emerge. But even with these domino-like effects of the Goldenberg fiasco dominating the news, its initiator was going on with his life hundreds of kilometres away without a clue. He partied with Kariuki, wooed Mariam and sold advertising space.

In spite of the busy days and wild nights, there is evidence that during this time, before he reappeared at Mariam's shop, David wanted to settle down. He had converted to Islam and approached two Muslim girls for their hand in marriage, only to be rejected. And that's why he suddenly appeared at Mariam's stall. The year was 1996. Mariam, who was not at her stall but down the street running an errand, remembers seeing David getting off a matatu. When he spotted her, he made a beeline for her. She was now 16.

'Salama lakini,' he said. Though taken aback at seeing him and wondering why he was there, Mariam immediately noticed that David had lost his brusque Baara edge over the past two years. From that point on, she convinced herself that he was from the Coast after all. Truth is appearance. To Mariam, David was a Mbarawa, a Coastal person of Somali origins. It made her burgeoning feelings for him somehow less outrageous.

Mariam noted his discomfort, like all women do of men who approach them seeking to express their affections – she held back her laughter as he blurted out that he wanted to talk to her. For a long time memories of the courtship would be a source of merriment for Mariam.

'Men! The ways of men are very strange! I looked at him and told him to come to my shop and tell me what he wanted. Us ... the way I've been raised, we don't believe in having too many stories when it comes to men and women, we believe in coming to the point straightaway. So I told him to come and see me again and tell me what he wanted.' Satisfied for the moment, David gratefully offered to buy her a soda in parting. She refused: 'Nilikataa kuchukua pesa kutoka mwanaume. Siwezi,' Mariam would say later during interviews. I couldn't accept anything from a man who had not declared himself.

Like any young girl being asked for her hand in marriage, a part of Mariam must have been thrilled, though she considered it unlikely they would end up together.

The next time David visited Mariam, she asked him about Janet, his one-time Taita girlfriend. He told Mariam he'd left Janet: 'Alikuwa anapenda pesa,' he said. He found her too materialistic. David probably saw his cue here and launched into what had brought him back to see Mariam. He told her how he had converted to Islam and was looking for a Muslim girl to marry and how he had been rejected by a certain Rehema. Would she, Mariam, be interested? Mariam, seeing he was serious, says: 'Tulikutana tuu mara mbili. Hii ndio mila yetu. Hakuna maneno mingi. Utasema vile unataka. Na kama kweli nakupenda basi ndakwambia huje nyumbani. Uongee na wazazi. Hakuna mastory mingi ya kupotezeana

29

wakati.' We had met twice. That was enough. With us Bajunis, you say what you want. No stories. And if you want to marry me and I like you, you go see my parents. No wasting each other's time.

David's friends were also aware that he had become a Muslim. But with them, this did not change his lifestyle. Kariuki laughs, saying, 'He became a Muslim of convenience. Nothing with us changed.'

Thus, the courtship started in earnest. From the moment he made his intentions clear, it would be unseemly for him to seek her out by himself: he would have to observe protocol and approach her through her sisters and parents. Once David showed Mariam a letter from the Kadhi attesting to his conversion to Islam and was introduced to her parents, he began paying regular visits to Mariam's sister's house, where his intended lived. He realised that she needed to get used to him, as he told her sister. He was ready to settle, and he was at a far more advanced emotional stage than her. It was not easy at first; Mariam, seeing him coming from a distance, would run off to friends' houses, perhaps bored stiff with what she probably saw as grown-up matters. David, who had been raised in the African Inland Church by his strict churchgoing grandmother, was probably attracted to Mariam because of her similarly strict religious background, albeit Muslim. The Bajun are a highly ritualised community like the Maasai, and though the two are as different as chalk and cheese, part of David recognised, admired and identified with these similarities.

Like many 16 year-old girls, Mariam was entranced by fictional worlds and escapist romances. She loved

Hollywood movies, and before David had made his intentions clear and his visits to woo Mariam had started, her life had been pretty straightforward. After a day at the stall, she would spend most evenings at a friend's house watching videos. Once David came into her life, it was hard to change immediately but her sister, noticing this game of panya na paka (cat and mouse), chided her. She advised David to select his visiting hours accordingly. Things smoothed out and the two became close. Now and then, David would find a few young men outside the house chatting to Mariam and watching him out of the corner of her eye, she would pretend to be oblivious of his jealousy. It was also a test. Mariam still harboured doubts about him – thinking he wasn't really interested in marrying her, that he wanted to bed her. The doubts were mostly about his break-up with Janet, whom she was still curious about.

'Alikuwa akiumia sana akiniona na marafiki wangu wengine,' she laughs. 'It was obvious it hurt him to see I had so many male friends.'

David also had some competition – a Tanzanian youth called Farisada who was closer to Mariam in age and in heart. The next five months would play a large role in David's success for the hand of Mariam. In the end, it came down to who could pay the bride-price first. In Bajun culture, with Ksh 30,000 and furniture for the parents, you get the girl. David got there first.

After a year or so, the two were like an engaged couple. Mariam says she started missing him and would call him if she didn't hear from him for even eight hours. All the while, no-one had realized David's true origins. Even the sister whom Mariam lived with and perhaps

31

the most worldly person in the family, would be shocked
to find out later that David was a Maasai. David, after
close to three years in Mombasa, had shape shifted into
a Mbarawa. David would later respond to this identity
confusion in a telling way. A very Kenyan way: 'It's
like when I tell people I'm a Maasai - and they say no.
I've learned, you see, that you don't have to tell people
anything. Wanakataa. Wanasema, how come? Hata
Mombasa I didn't have to tell them anything, no? They
said I was a Mbarawa, they did not know any Maasais.'

At the wedding, only David's brother, Daniel, and
the latter's father-in-law were present. The men from
Mariam's family wore kikois and rubber-thonged
sandals on their feet and the women were in black
veils with only their eyes visible to the world. The
bridegroom's family was represented by only two men:
brother Dan Munyakei, darker than David, looking
like the prosperous Limuru bank officer he still is. He
wore the standard Nairobi visitor's attire at the coast,
touristy, uncomfortable looking. Daniel's father-in-law
was wearing a suit as is the wont of older Kenyan men.
Daniel says: 'We mostly just sat there. There was a lot
of respect for us. We were served by women on their
knees. I don't remember anyone asking us where we
were from.' Daniel does not seem surprised that his new
in-laws did not know their origins and laughs. 'Hiyo
maneno sijui. I was only involved at the wedding and did
not know my brother's relations with his wife. Even him
becoming a Muslim, we only knew about much later.'

Mariam says in a retrospective tone of amazement:
'Siku ya harusi tulishangaa kile hawa watu walikuwa
wakiongea. Na ilikuwa Kikuyu tu, je ingeje ingelikuwa
Kimaasai? Familia yetu tulikuwa wengi. Kwao ilikuwa guka

tu na baba Liz. Hatukufuatilia sana kwani yeye alisema mamake aliaga, babake hakuwa wa ndoa nako Olokurto ni mbali sana watu wa kwao kuja Mombasa.Tulidhani kakake ni mtu wa Mombasa ametoka kazini. Tulikaa sana kabla tujue kweli huyu si mtu wa pwani. Nilishangaa sana, sikuwa nimeishika hiyo accent.' We wondered what these people were speaking. It turned out to be Kikuyu. What if it had been Maasai? I would never have married him! Maasai sounds so harsh.   A large part of our family was present. Raju said that he had been born out of wedlock and had no father. His family was his brother and his brother's father-in-law. We felt pity for David as his mum was dead and didn't question him when he said his relatives were far away. We thought his brother was working in Mombasa. Later on, discovering everything was a shock - even the accent I hadn't gotten yet.

The young couple got married in 1997 and soon David started seeking a permanent job. With a family, David felt that he could not afford to rely on the vicissitudes and unreliability of sales earnings. Luck was with him, he would say later, and he landed a job as sales manager at a large furniture dealer with a monthly salary.

David Sadera Munyakei also known as Rajab, for the second time in his life found himself in the centre of a web of corruption. Immigration and Customs at the Mombasa port has consistently featured in the top five of all lists of corruption drawn up by corruption watchdogs. All through the 1990s, corruption at the port was at its most rampant. The Kenya Revenue Authority (KRA) had just been formed and at the time was based at the Mombasa port. David would later say the furniture company was into serious tax-evasion and bribery. And

33

he found himself, as a sales manager, in charge of clearing the company's furniture imports.

'I was told not to worry when I got to Customs. Everything was taken care of.' And indeed the imports went through without paying any duties. It became clear to David what was happening when a senior KRA official came into the showroom and started selecting the most exclusive pieces of furniture, then left without paying a cent. Taken aback, David must have started asking questions as his bosses sent him to their office in Nairobi for a 're-education' in how Kenya worked. After a week, he came back to Mombasa resolved to turn a blind eye to what was going on – after all, he had two mouths at home to feed. But even with his compliance, it soon became evident to the authorities what was going on at the port; the senior official was fired and KRA eventually closed down the furniture company along with other scapegoats.

Once again, David was out of a job. Mombasa, in spite of its size, works like a small town, and given this high turnover of jobs, doors started closing for David. Now that the dream had died, he was forced to look far over the horizon, hundreds of kilometres away, to the place where he had come from so long ago. A place he at times referred to as 'home' and as 'that place' according to his mood. He spent nights staring at the ceiling searching for answers with his young wife sleeping peacefully next to him. The thought of going back to Olokurto must have been galling. Later, David would say that the best years of his life were those he spent in Mombasa. But the reality at the time was that he was unemployed and he had a family. For any Kenyan man who has left his rural home, there is an implied failure in going back to mashambani when still relatively young, and this must have cut David to the quick. But part of him realised that the Maasai nation was the only place he could go back to and regroup. He was lucky that he had a nation to fall back on. Many young men in Kenya's urban areas did not have a tangible tribal framework to support them after the effects of the gradual collapse of the Moi State had caught up with them. Munyakei would be embraced and taken in like the prodigal son by the Maasai nation. There, he would be safe from the hardships of the larger Kenya. He could return from his self-exile. The light-skinned young man who had got off the bus four years ago now boarded one in the other direction. He was now heavier and lighter-skinned than before, and had a wife and baby in tow. He had also acquired a Muslim identity, Rajab or Raju as his wife affectionately called him. It might have occurred to him he would have to revert back to an earlier identity to survive where they were going. So they boarded a Coast Bus and headed 'home' - a place in Narok District, 5,000 feet above sea level, called Olokurto (pronounced Olo Ku-rrr-tho). Mariam, still oblivious to who her Raju really was, would go through a re-education of sorts. It would be quite a while before she saw the sea, the sand and the palm trees she had been accustomed to seeing all her life.

Part 2:
Olokurto/Narok -The Formative Years and the Return of the Native

'The state of the native is a nervous condition.'

(Frantz Fanon, The Wretched of the Earth)

IT WAS IN LATE 1998 that David arrived with his new family at Olokurto. Visits to the place of his origins had been irregular and short up to then - the last time he had been to Olokurto was 1996. He had not lived there for at least 17 years. Yet this was the place where the Munyakei family had lived for possibly four generations. Definitely three, according to a first-hand account by the oldest living Munyakei family member, David's grandmother Milka.

In 1937, a young Kikuyu girl named Milka Wambui left Kiambu, Central Province, then known as Kabete, and moved to Kijabe, Rift Valley with her family. Even back then, migration out of Central Province for different reasons was not unheard of. The Kikuyu were highly mobile as a tribe by virtue of their social organisation, which had been shaped by the necessity of seeking new lands to cultivate, especially after the loss of their lands in the colonial era. In Kijabe, Milka Wambui met and married a

Maasai man named Hosea Munyakei. The couple moved to Subukia to start a new life. The peaceful rusticity they settled into was disrupted like that of many Africans when the state of Emergency was declared in 1952. Africans were asked to return to their native homes so the couple moved back to Olokurto, Narok, Hosea Munyakei's home village. By and by three daughters were born to Hosea and Milka - Sarah Koikoi, Elizabeth Sembeyo and Emily Munyakei. Hosea was not to live to a ripe old age like his wife Milka; he died in 1967. By this time, the girls were grown up and had launched out in different careers - Elizabeth, David's mother, joined the Prisons Department in the 1960s.

In 1965, she gave birth to a son named Daniel Munyakei. Our David, David Sadera Munyakei, was born three years later. The two boys were born of different fathers. Both were born out of wedlock. Elizabeth Sembeyo, who died in 1993, is described in glowing terms by all those who knew her.

Hardworking and responsible, she is said to have gone the extra financial mile for any of her extended family. By the time she passed from the stage, she was the main breadwinner of the extended Munyakei family. On meeting the younger sister, Emily Munyakei, who their mother Milka says resembles the late Elizabeth, one gets a sense of David's late mother. Light-skinned, short and opinionated, Emily is direct in a very disarming way - she is an example of Gikuyu frontier womanhood straight out of the Wangu wa Makeri legend. A woman who can raise a family, farm, run a business and take care of her ageing mother, all without the help of a man. Like many people of mixed ethnicity in Narok and Maasailand, one of her favourite topics is Maasai politics and the election in 2007, on which she is full of insights and analyses that you will never read in the mainstream press.

Emily's sister, Elizabeth Sembeyo, lived with her

sons in Langata Prisons, where she was stationed until an order for a transfer to Narok came through in 1974. David Sadera was six years old. His earliest memories of childhood in Langata are of mud huts, nyumba za matope. David would later recount how the family spoke Swahili and Maasai, rarely Kikuyu, which they spoke when his maternal aunts came to visit. And that was mostly between the boys' mother and her sisters. Their life in Langata was interrupted when Elizabeth Sembeyo was transferred to Narok. This would not be the only transfer in her career and she asked her mother Milka, who was still in Olokurto, to take care of her two boys. Daniel went first and David followed when he was six. Elizabeth Sembeyo built a wooden house for her mother and the two boys to live in. This is the house David Sadera Munyakei would live in till he passed on. The two boys joined a nearby school, Olokurto Primary, and perhaps because of the culture shock, David's most poignant childhood memories would reside in the Olokurto of his boyhood, which he would remember, years later, with characteristic wryness: 'It was a bit hard, but when you are a child, adjusting is not very difficult. I cannot remember much of Langata. There were mud houses for staff.'

Daniel, being older, remembers much more of the time before Olokurto than David.

'Mimi nilienda kwanza kuiishi na cucu. David alienda na mathe Nakuru.

Halafu mama akamleta akiwa mdogo.

Daniel refers to Olokurto as 'our place' in his incessant comparisons with Limuru, where he has lived for the past five years, and where you have to lock your doors, live next to people who are not really your neighbours and be prepared for the possibility that bad things can happen to you at anytime. And this is without talking of Nairobi, which he can't stand.

The brothers thus adapted to Olokurto.

'In Olokurto maisha ilikuwa ngumu. Life was very hard. Hapa nilikuja kuaanza kuchunga kondoo… nini. Kulima. Maisha ilikuwa tofauti. Nilikuwa nikilima. Kuangalia kondoo kabla uende shule. Ukichelewa, mwalimu anakuchapa,' David would remember.

'You leave school even at 1, unaambiwa upeleke maziwa. When you come back from school, you have to go and dig. It was very rough but very educative in the sense that you got to know real life.'

Apart from the physical discomfort, there was also the question of adapting to a new culture - that of the Maasai nation: 'We were not outsiders, but at the same time we did not follow the Maasai culture because we were a bit civilised. We were not all that local … adjusting to the local community took a long time.'

David talked of his place in the Maasai nation without any sense of irony. Like most Kikuyus or people of mixed ethnicity who have lived in Maasailand and intermarried and acquired some Maasai customs, he could not escape the feeling of 'otherness.' Even having prospered and benefited from the Maasai nation, many Kikuyu still frown on Maasai ways - wearing blankets, living in manyattas, skipping the odd bath and the whole nomadic lifestyle. Maasais who have left their homelands and gone to the city and received a formal education integrating them into 'modern' Kenya also shun the old ways. John Keen famously threatened to resign as a Maasai leader in the 1970s if the Maasai did not stop showing their buttocks to the whole world. Maasais who can read and write, referred to as waliosoma (those who are educated) still look askance at those who wear blankets and have never seen the inside of a classroom, the wamashuka, (those who wear sheets), and vice versa.

The divisions among the Maasai do not end there; you have the so-called Maasai purebloods and those who have intermarried with other tribes, mostly the Kikuyu, and are referred to as half-bloods. The purebloods frown on the Kikuyu-isms that have infiltrated their half-blood cousins. These, as perceived by the wamashuka, range from wearing a suit or 'modern clothes' to eating roast goat with ugali. The signs of being an 'impure' Maasai are many, varied, and subtle, and those who are half-bloods are referred to as Ole Mereki (pronounced Mereghi) which means 'foreigner' or simply Kikuyu.

But this does not mean that outsiders are unwelcome. The Maasai way of life is very accommodating of those who take to it without reservation. The story of a young man who once lived in one of the most remote areas in Kenya, a place called Mosiro in Narok District, is often told to illustrate this principle. They called him Ole Karanja there. Ole Karanja was once David Karanja, born and bred in Southlands, Langata in Nairobi. He had attended St. George's Primary School and later Strathmore School. At the age of 20, he found himself at odds with the law and his father, who was half Maasai, half Kikuyu, and had 'friends' drive him to Mosiro. He was taken by his new friends into Tanzania and lived with a Maasai community there till things cooled down. After that, he came back to Mosiro and started a new life, setting up a small shop. In time, he became integrated into the community and was 'given' a woman. He also got a piece of land from his new father-in-law. Five years later, he is fully a Mosiro 'Maasai,' observing all their customs and leading their way of life like any other 'pureblood.' He, however, travels outside the Maasai nation to Nairobi for business once in a while and at times goes to eat and drink at Carnivore, in remembrance of his late teens when he

41

lived in Langata. If you find him there he is David Karanja, St. George's, Strath, because he is outside his nation and is in 'Kenya.' And you can never tell he is a shopkeeper in Mosiro.

The story of David Munyakei is slightly different; it is perhaps not very surprising that as somebody who is only part Maasai, he often said: 'No, I can never adapt to the Maasai lifestyle even though I now appreciate the life.

'There are some things that you cannot do,' he said, 'like living in the Maasai manyattas, living in the skin, wearing blankets. Like now, you come and find me wearing a blanket or a shuka and no underwear. You know. You appreciate the lifestyle but you cannot do such things.' Adding somewhat facetiously: 'Ndi Mugikuyu. Nie Ndi Mugikuyu.'

This world-view was probably acquired from his grandmother, who is a full Kikuyu, and as she explains: 'Tulikuwa mbele. Tulikuwa wachristo wa AIC. Hata hiyo maneno ya ki-Islamu hatuijui.' We were more advanced [than the Maasai]. We were AIC Christians. Even this business of Islam [David Munyakei's conversion in Mombasa], I don't know what that is all about.

His brother Daniel gives a less insular version of their childhood, recognising that there was a strong Maasai influence to it all. 'We were Maasai through and through, hata kama masikio haikupasuliwa na hatukuvaa mashuka.' Even though we didn't pierce our ears and wear blankets. He says that their home area per se was not deeply Maasai as there were other influences.

'Mostly, where we live now, KiMaasai per se is not regarded as deep because of school life. But we used to go inside where there were no schools and we would see that deep Maasai life. We knew, understood and appreciated that life. We used to understand them but we also went to school.'

42

David's grandmother, Milka, says he was just like any other boy - he went out grazing cattle and climbed trees. When the time came, he was baptised in the AIC church at a stream near the Munyakei home and named David. But in spite of all these other identities, David Munyakei is also Maasai. He was born in Maasailand, spoke Maasai. Anywhere outside of Maasailand, his accent and manner would immediately mark where he came from.

The Maasai have always had a parallel system of government to the colonial and post-colonial administrations. Till today, there endures a largely invisible system of justice with unwritten laws that is highly effective and is left well alone by the government in Nairobi. A council of elders in each clan presides over the Maasai nation in federal fashion. In the Maasai nation, Government of Kenya-appointed administrators wield little real power. The power is held by locally elected officials like councillors, who respect the old ways.

When a Maasai breaks a law within their system of justice - even if it is murder - justice is meted out according to Maasai law. The police are rarely called in. This works well for all involved till Maasai ways clash with Kenyan law. For example, the Maasai have never held title deeds. Land ownership is determined through borders called mpakas, like rivers or trees. However, all land can be used by all Maasais for grazing and trespass is a foreign concept. Those Maasai who in times of drought come in from the Athi Plains and graze their cows at the airport often argue that planes do not eat grass and there is therefore no reason that their cows should starve. Bamburi Portland Cement's plant at Athi River often encounters the same cultural snafu when Maasais bring their cows into its compounds.

'Our cows do not eat limestone,' the Maasais tell

them over and over again. Maasais believe in something
called engoki, a curse or nemesis that befalls those who
do wrong. The belief in engoki ensures that the Maasai
refrain from wronging anyone. From this stems the basic
honesty of the Maasai that is totally at odds with the larger
Kenya. This honesty and straightforwardness is perceived
by the larger Kenya to be at best a lack of street smarts
and, at worst, outright stupidity. Among the Kikuyu it is a
constant refrain: stop acting like a Maasai.

Among other Maasai ways that outsiders find strange
is the famous one of women not being allowed to eat
with men. In Narok, one finds segregated restaurants
with different sections for men and women. In places
that do not observe this custom, Maasai men leave their
women outside as they eat. There is also the Maasai army,
the morans, as well as their medicinemen, the olaiboni
who exist to this very day as their clinics and hospitals.
The educated and formally employed are the upper-
class citizens of the Maasai nation. Though Maasai self-
awareness and sense of belonging to a tangible nation has
been present since the earliest historical accounts of the
Maasai (the Maasai sent a separate delegation to negotiate
with the British before independence) it was massively
reinforced in the national consciousness during the Moi
years. The 1980s and 90s saw the growth of tribalism in
Kenya. Many Kenyans fell back on tribal ways to redefine
themselves in a Kenya where the nation state had suffered
a tremendous attrition. Suddenly people did not define
themselves as Kenyans but as members of their tribe
first.

During independence negotiations, the British
proposed a concept of Kenya as a contractual state
comprising different ethnic nations. Once Kenyatta was
in power, the lines between these nations became blurred

with that of the emerging state of Kenya. The major tribes' interests were one with the emerging Kenya and it was not in the Kikuyu interest to have recognisable tribal nations. As the Meru-based writer Paul Goldsmith points out: 'There have been different degrees of growth in the social development of tribes in Kenya because of different reasons, not least proximity to political power. Decades of spatial separation widened the socio-economic gap separating agricultural and pastoral communities, which in turn morphed into post-independence social exclusion.' Over time, excluded nations such as the Pokot, Turkana and Maasai have come to refer to the rest of the country as 'Kenya.' 'Umetoka Kenya?' one is often asked when entering Pokot, Turkana or remote Maasailand.

Maasais have always defined themselves by a set of unique customs and circumcision is an integral part of being Maasai. Munyakei was circumcised under the ngilishi age-group and, like all young Maasai men, taught the ways of his tribe during the initiation period. A large part of Munyakei's identity as a Maasai must have been imbibed then.

Still, David would say, 'It was very rough – even at school. Wakisema wee ni mzungu utasema nini?' If the children at school say you are white, what do you say back to them? The taunts all through school continued into adulthood; up to the day of his death, everyone outside his family in the Olokurto Trading Centre referred to him as Ole Shumbai, a part derogatory, part affectionate term meaning white man. At times his Olokurto Trading Centre acquaintances called him Ole Mereki. Kikuyu.

Olokurto today remains a remote place. To get there, you turn off the road between Narok town and Nakuru just before you get to Ole Tipis, where the road climbs into the Mau Narok Hills. You pass trading centres with names like Olopito, Eor-Okitok, Kisiriri, Enaibelbel, Olokirikirai, Lengetia, Naitupaki, Enarau, Medungi, all the way to Olokurto Trading Centre. As bad as the road to Narok is, it is nothing compared with the one to Olokurto, which is basically a river of dust. Dust so fine that it seeps into your sealed car, so thick it is like a mattress. When the rutted road finally breaks the universal joint of your car and you attempt to fix it, this is the dust you lie in. (When it rains the rivers of dust become rivers of mud, and there is no public transport between Olokurto and Narok.) Your eyelashes soon become brown and you sneeze hard enough for your eyes to pop out and to lose some of your brain matter as mucus. On this river of dust, all the way stations you pass look the same; you wonder what was going through Mariam's mind as the young family made this final passage on their exodus from Mombasa in 1998.

Goldsmith has also observed that remote pastoral communities, while seen by most Kenyans as being held back by anti-progressive cultural forces, are in the eyes of the tourist the stuff of postcard images, of colourful tribesmen, dramatic landscapes and abundant wildlife. It is said that the road to Narok, (the one tourists use to get to the Mara) was left as it is to create the effect of being remote. A common saying in the area is that in the Mara, wanyama count for more than human beings.

Olokurto has the ramshackle front of trading centres all over Kenya. Behind this almost Wild West false front are numerous small wooden bars with names like Top Life and Good Hope Maasai Bar whose proprietors are Kikuyu; rooms to let the size of large dog-kennels; wooden pool rooms; chai and mandazi cafes; flimsy pit latrines and more and more of the bars one sees all over Maasailand. The claustrophobia of these tiny rooms is a huge contrast to the Olokurto sky, the biggest you'll ever see in Kenya. Like Graham Greene's descriptions of the places he visited in Kenya in the 1950's, Olokurto is a 'sky-wrapped land.' All faint blue if it's early morning, with frost on the ground if it's July. Even in January, it is still cold enough in the early morning for you to feel as if your ears are flapping. It is said that it gets so cold in Olokurto that children do not grow.

This is mostly barley, sheep and wheat country, in that order, and they harvest later than all wheat growing regions in Kenya. In January, the fields will be green and gold as Olokurto's (mostly Kikuyu, almost exclusively non-Maasai) farmers wait for their wheat to dry. To the east of Olokurto lies Ole Tipis, to the west Olenguruone. To the north you find Nyahururu and Njoro and to the south Olepinok. The countryside is beautiful: a rolling landscape of russets, blues and greens. The light is what a painter would call hard, a quality found in places that straddle the equator.

It is at the trading centre that you will see the most people. Generally idlers, they sit there watching the cars passing and point far in the distance, laughing: 'Ule mjinga anangojea nini-hiyo ngano iko tayari kuvunwa.' That fool, I don't know what he's waiting for -that wheat is ready for harvest. They will laugh, hawk and clear their throats and plant a gob of spit in the dust.

The Munyakei homestead is a 20-minute walk from the trading centre and after becoming the 'Goldenberg whistleblower' David Munyakei was used to receiving many visitors. There are fewer people on the way to the home than the trading centre. If it is the middle of the day, you'll be lucky to meet anyone you can ask for directions - maybe a solitary child, all giggly and shy with eyes as big as the sky. Or a young herdsman lying by the side of the road with a shoot of grass sticking out of his mouth. More often than not he'll have flipped his shuka aside to sun his balls. He will observe you without the slightest curiosity on his face.

The wooden front house where David Munyakei received his guests is Spartan, containing a small sitting room and three even smaller bedrooms. The kitchen is a small hut behind the front house, and it is there his mother and her sisters grew up. Smoke winds its way into the blue sky from the hut. Inside the sitting room, there are ornamental horned skulls and animal charts hanging on the wall for his children. The furniture is functional - 1970s 'jumbo' button leather seats and small wooden tables. Outside, there is a small hobbit-like grass mound, beneath which there is a colony of termites. Many a visitor has been subjected to their attentions while talking to David and looking amazedly at the huge sky.

'Hii siafu ndio inanichunga,' David once said to me with a rare laugh after I suddenly jumped up and yelled from ant bites. These ants are here to watch over me.

This is where David ended up with his family after quitting Mombasa in 1998, having left it in 1981 when he joined Narok High School, later going onto Chavakali Secondary School, schools his brother had also attended. When the couple and their child arrived, David Munyakei's grandmother Milka took them in. Milka remembers thinking how young Mariam looked. She also remembers noticing that her grandson Sadera and his new bride did not have basic farming skills. David would explain how they made do: 'We just did what everybody did.' The learning curve was not without its comic moments. Mariam, who had never in her life known where crop foods came from, would harvest potatoes and put back the potato stalk in the soil thinking that another potato would grow from it. Other rural chores like looking for firewood were difficult: 'Nilijaribu kukata mti kwa shoka nikashindwa. Baba Naima ndiye huuni vunjia miti. Nimejaribu kukata miti kama mara kumi.Nashangaa sana Cucu hubeba kuni, kama ingekuwa mama yangu angekuwa amekufa.' I tried to cut wood with an axe; I couldn't do it. I must have tried 10 times. Baba Naima [David] used to do it for me. I was amazed to see Cucu [grandmother] carrying huge bundles of firewood with ease; if it was my own mother, she would have dropped dead on the spot.

This was the least of her problems. She says she was often bored, especially on Sundays when Gogo (a Maasai term for grandmother), left for her AIC service. Her greatest fear was the Warani, young Maasai morans who visit homesteads to ask for milk and meat as dictated by tradition. These particular ones are said to have come from the forest as far away as Kajiado. Harmless to pureblood Maasais, Warani seek out non-Maasai homesteads and subject them to varying degrees of harassment - from demanding milk to stealing livestock to gorge themselves with in the forest. At times they came on Sundays, when Mariam was alone, and she often feared she would be raped. She could hear them from a distance as the Warani were given to wailing, ululating and roaring like lions.

'Walikuwa wakikuja wakikoroma.' They came roaring.

Maasai and non-Maasai live deeply different parallel lives in Maasailand.

Any Maasai will tell you the Warani are harmless, but Mariam claims that they stole livestock from the Munyakei homestead and killed the cow she had been given as bride-price by David's family. The Warani are rural but like the Mungiki, they are known to forcibly kidnap young Maasai men to propagate the old ways. The Warani are in the moran stage, the warrior rite of passage that comes after circumcision and lasts for at least two years.

One day in 2000, the Warani appeared and found Mariam with Gogo Munyakei. Immediately the warriors saw the old woman, they turned around and left, afraid that she would either curse or cast a spell on them. Mariam says they never came to the Munyakei homestead again.

It took Mariam two years to adapt to living in Olokurto. At one point, she even went back home to Lamu and refused to come back to her husband. David had to travel to the Coast to fetch her, but she refused to go with him, so he took his first daughter Naima away. His grandmother sent him back after another three months. Mariam again refused to return, but after another two months, missing her only child, she sent for David to come and fetch her. After that, she managed to learn to live in Olokurto and has over time come to love it. It took a while before she got used to walking long distances, and the idea of men wearing sheets and blankets. Olokurto was very different from Mombasa, where people take matatus for distances as little as 50 metres.

'Mombasa jua kali, joto, bahari... Watu huko hatutembei. Nilipokuja hapa nakuanza kutembea, nilikuwa nahema!' she laughs. 'Imagine baba Naima alikuwa anabook matatu ikuje kunichukuwa hapa. Sikuweza kutemebea hadi trading centre kama tunasafiri. Marafiki wanakaa mbali. Kama ningekuwa Mombasa, ningechukuwa mathree kobole mpaka dukani. Mombasa kila pahali kuna matatu.' Mombasa is hot, it's on the Coast. People there don't walk. I came here and I had to walk everywhere. I would be panting after a few minutes. I couldn't even walk to the trading centre like we've just done. Everyone you know stays so far away, to visit with friends you just have to walk. In Mombasa, I thought nothing of spending five shillings on a matatu just to go down to the shops. In

Mombasa, you can get a matatu anywhere. She could not understand how anyone could eat so much meat. She had been used to a diet of coconut rice supplemented with fish, the staple food of the Coast. She was always amazed at the Maasai habit of drinking raw goat lard, often tipping up a full cup and draining it in one long draught. She would watch in alarm as Gogo gave her only child lard to drink. She says: 'Gogo alikuwa anakunywa mafuta kwa kikombe. Huyu Naima alipewa mafuta na cream na cucu mpaka kazoea.' Gogo would drink goat fat from a cup herself, and give it to Naima mixed with cream until the child got used to the taste. Life was hard, and at times the family had to go without bread and sugar. In the early days, Mariam hardly left her room, and would often receive with shock nothing but a cup of sugarless black tea for breakfast. Outside the planting and harvesting seasons, Mariam staved off boredom by teaching young Muslims in the area the Quran and listening to the radio for hours on end. She was unable to learn Maa, though her children speak it. Her once sanifu Swahili became peppered with Kikuyu expressions. She became fond of exclaiming Ngai and using words like iriga, which means fence, a concept that probably does not have a Lamu Swahili equivalent since it is largely foreign to that culture. Her mongrelised Kiswahili made her an object of derision when she went back to the Coast, with her nephews and nieces openly laughing at her. Her sister often berated her, asking her to stop speaking like a Mmbaara in front of neighbours and friends.

Mariam made quite a sight, making her way through the Olokurto countryside dressed in her buibui. Kids went crazy, jumping up and down when she passed, and her own children, who understand Maa, told her: 'Mummy, hawa watoto wanakutukana. Wanakuita paka!' These children are insulting you. They are calling you a black cat.

Over time, the couple learnt how to farm, with David starting on one side of a field and she on the other - and they managed to survive. Now she proudly says that the maize she farmed in a previous year would last the family the whole year.

This was the kind of existence David Munyakei led when the government changed in 2002 and President Kibaki subsequently formed a commission to get to the root of the Goldenberg matter. Munyakei voluntarily travelled to Nairobi to introduce himself to the Goldenberg Commission. Things had come full circle. Ten years earlier, he had fled Nairobi, now he returned there with a sense of triumph and the hope that justice would finally prevail. He was to be disappointed. Like many Kenyans, he learnt that the fruits of Kenya, in the minds of our new leaders, only belong to the few who have always enjoyed them.

Years earlier, in the early 1980s, in a strange twist of fate, another man running away from a different kind of state-related persecution had also hidden in the Munyakeis' Olokurto home. His name was Koigi wa Wamwere and this was just after the 1982 coup. Munyakei's grandmother Milka Wambui is related to the famous politician's mother. Daniel remembers Koigi living with them when Daniel was in his last years in primary school. He remembers how a young Koigi disguised himself to fool the police, who several times came right to the Munyakeis' doorstep. Years later, Munyakei would emulate Koigi, though he hardly had the luxury of fleeing to Norway.

Part 3:
Nairobi: Do Not Be Green in the
City in the Sun. Kula Pesa ya Pattni!

*I was trying to draw the attention of the government as I
initially thought that the government was not aware what was
going on at the CBK.*

(David Munyakei's thoughts when he blew the whistle on Goldenberg)

TWELVE YEARS AGO, before David Munyakei's
life turned on itself, he had come to Nairobi as a young
man with a sense of entitlement and great plans for the
future. His high school record was exemplary and he was
someone who had held positions of responsibility in both
his O level and A level schools. Before Munyakei was
offered employment at the CBK he had also been accepted
as a cadet in the Army. He ws planning on accepting when
the CBK offer came through and he opted instead to
become a banker.

After being in the service of the State in a uniform, his
mother felt this had more attractions than a career in the
service of the State, and also an opportunity for someone
in the family to branch out. 'It was only one year after
leaving school in 1989 when I joined Central Bank. I had

just come back to Nairobi. My initial ambition was to join the army and I went for recruitment and qualified as a cadet officer. Along the way before I could join the force we decided that not all of us were for the force,' Munyakei said.

CBK positions were prestigious and difficult to come by. Munyakei knew that the job also included opportunities for further studies: 'I applied for my job and I was qualified and I was employed in the proper procedure. I went for all the tests and I qualified.'

So he joined the CBK in 1991. The Central Bank is both a citadel and behemoth; its design communicates all the finesse of muscle. Until the late 1990s, the Bank building dominated Haile Selassie Avenue. Then Times Tower was completed, all 30 storeys of it. Now the two, with their constant supply of armed guards, dominate the street like bullies at the back of the class. Somewhere inside the Central Bank is the Development Department where Munyakei started working in 1991. Created in 1966, the CBK is a hierarchical institution, an offspring of the Bretton Woods philosophy that created financial institutions central to the economy of developing countries back in the 1950'sand 1960's. At the head of the Central Bank of Kenya is the Governor – a position curious in the government bureaucracy because of its power and autonomy, like being both CEO and chairman of the board. The Governor is a Presidential appointee but with security of tenure. In Moi times, the Governor was directly answerable to the President. In Kibaki's different ruling style, the position pays allegiance to the Finance Minister.

A CBK insider who has worked in mostly senior positions since the 1990's describes the institutional philosophy of the organization: 'Mediocrity is the single most obvious character trait at CBK. And this shows itself through the single most important trait, and this is misplaced loyalty, loyalty to individuals, not commitment to banking rules, regulation and practice.' He adds: 'There is a chain of inter-linkages formed from the bottom to the top, especially in departments where money flows. If you are out of favour you are relegated to the so called non-cash departments. Things haven't really changed since Pattni and there is still an Old Boy network with those who really benefited still in place.' At the CBK the Pattni times are still remembered with fondness. Many are still living off pesa ya Pattni.

So this was the kind of place David Sadera Munyakei, a young man with large ambitions, found himself: 'When I went to the Central Bank I was supposed to go to college but it was decided that this young man should be recruited at the Central Bank and after three years that he should be given a scholarship because he was qualified to go to university. I was very qualified to study economics and it was agreed by the bank that I should be recruited and after three years I should be given a scholarship which is within the banking provisions for training. That's why I joined the central bank; otherwise I wanted first to go to school and finish my education, get my degree, get my Masters degree, get my PhD degree and now come and settle.' But though this did not come to pass, David immediately realized he was lucky to get the job. It is not clear whether he got the job without any political canvassing - a cousin claims that David got the job through the influence of the man David would claim is his father, a local Maasai politician.

David would deny this, saying he got the job fair and square, an unlikely occurrence but not impossible. Among his colleagues were State Comptroller Franklin Bett's wife, and the daughter of Moi's driver. David conceded that 'there was a lot of political patronage,' adding: 'If you were qualified you could easily get the job. I was very happy because my ambitions were very high. I had a very big vision. I joined banking in 1991. I admired banking and decided to be a banker. It is a suitable profession. Okay especially at that time. It was also a place where one could advance.'

Like many boys, David had always wanted to become a pilot when he grew up. Now 23, he was a clerk in the Central Bank. The boy's dreams had been replaced by the man's need to survive in the real world, in Nairobi. 'After completing school things change. Reality changed. Becoming a pilot was a childish dream,' he would say.

By coming to Nairobi, Munyakei had stepped way outside the protection of the Maasai nation where he had grown up. Though he realized there were different rules to Nairobi and the larger Kenya he probably didn't realise the degree to which this was a reality. This has happened to many a Maasai who has had dealings outside the Maasai nation.

'I was very happy at the Central Bank when I started and I was very young. I joined CBK and only knew something was wrong after a whole year. I realized that something was wrong … the working procedures. Something was not right.'

The following is an unedited transcript of David Sadera Munyakei's recorded account of what took place from the time he discovered something was wrong in the Department he worked for, then exposing it and being arrested. It also contains his account of fleeing Nairobi for Mombasa.

Munyakei: When I realized things were not right I consulted Onyango Jamasai who was a friend of mine.

He was senior and was available. I often discussed with him what was going on and he agreed that something was wrong. We would go out of work and socialize. We were very intimate. I could tell him these things. Jamasai said to me, 'These transactions are illegal. It's common sense: where does gold and diamonds come from in Kenya to warrant these millions? Please be careful.'

Apart from another man, Kiambati, who was also a friend, the atmosphere in the office was not very free. They [Njoroge and Sisenda, Munyakei's bosses] were a bit aloof. They were my bosses and they used to keep to themselves very much. Maybe by virtue of knowing what was going on. They were not open. Jamasai was very open. Njoroge and Sisenda had something to hide. I remember once when they had an argument about money in front of us. It was open corruption. They behaved like they didn't care. 'We are the bosses' they seemed to say. Hakuna pahali unaeza kunipeleka.

Everything happened for a long time, about one year. After '92 elections this thing became very rampant and became open stealing. I said no. I'd never told anyone, not even my brother. The only person I discussed this issue with was Onyango Jamasai and he was a stickler to the rules and regulations within the banking procedures. I could go to him and I liked him because he would tell me 'Munyakei this is wrong, and this is right.' Jamasai was a very diligent man. If something is wrong he could tell you to your face… And you know we were young and wanted to build our careers. We were aiming high and Onyango Jamasai was one of the people we would go to. I knew he was one of the people who could build somebody young like me. You cannot be built by somebody who is dishonest.

From high school I was given leadership because I

was honest and very loyal. There was no way I could do anything wrong. After 1992 elections things went haywire and there were no rules, no regulations. I said no this is wrong and after that Mr Kiambati who had actually been in the system, gave me alot of advice. I had consulted with the management and raised complaints, and they did nothing. I decided to go ahead and expose what was going on. I remember my colleagues asking me, 'Mister, where exactly is the gold you seem to be clearing?'

The joke became irritating.

We used to meet at Kiambati's office in Uchumi house, 6th floor. He had a tour firm. We agreed that the economy could not grow with this kind of thing happening, and we decided to approach the MPs. Kiambati introduced me to them. We met several times. I told Anyang' Nyong'o and Muite what was happening and after I gave them the proof they believed me, saying Kenya belonged to everyone and that this needed to be exposed.

I was trying to draw the attention of the government. I initially thought that the government was not aware what was going on at the CBK… I was not aware…I would come to learn later that this thing was a big thing.

It took three months after I met the MPs for the story to come out in the newspaper. I have never met Pattni. He did not talk to people like us. He was normally seen going to see the CBK Bank Secretary giving his secretary Kshs 20,000 for lunch. Pattni only talked to the governor. Njoroge and Sisenda, my bosses, were not open. If you took anything to them they would tell you to go ahead and process it. Them, they knew what was going on. You being down there, you wouldn't know. They would tell you to ignore. You are told to ignore. I used to drink everyday because of stress. The moment I leave the office I leave work. I never told anybody what was going on. I used to go out weekends to drink.

Kiambati must be the one who gave Warutere the information. What I thought and what I expected is that the beneficiaries of the scheme will follow the rules and regulations of the scheme. And that the culprits will desist from doing what they were doing. When I saw the newspaper I was very very happy. I even talked to people in my office about it. We were several in the department. I showed the whole department. On processing the vouchers, I did the most though Esther Karimi and Mrs Bett, also clerks, would do it when I asked for help. Nobody reacted to the newspaper story. It didn't last two days. There is a lady who came and told me that she had heard a rumour but everything in that story was correct.

So after there was a big story, to cover up the CID were ordered to investigate. Wakauliza hii kazi inafanywa kwa department gani. Kukuja kwa department wakauliza hii kazi inafanywa na nani. Wakaambiwa ni Munyakei. They were talking to the bosses. Sisenda and Njoroge told them it was Munyakei who did this and that's what happens when you go to a department and need to know what goes on. So that's when they came to arrest me. They came to the head of department and they were told it is Munyakei and since I had been complaining they knew and were not happy.

Are you getting me?

If you are head of department, you know everything.

Some CBK security officers found me at the canteen and told me that I was wanted at the security office at CBK. I didn't know why they wanted me. I met two gentlemen, one was called Mr Macharia. Brown and of average height. The head of security Mr Karanja told me I was under arrest. Under arrest for what? It was then that things changed...It's like I tell you ebu kuja kidogo and on reaching outside nikudunge kisu! It was such a surprise! I asked them what's happening they could not talk and told me we "Twende kwanza, tutaongea mbele." CID headquarters.

Along the way it's when they told me 'Ohhh it has been claimed that you are the person communicating with members of the Opposition. You are the one who is giving them information.' 'Kuenda tuu. No interrogation. So I stayed there for a whole day. I just sat in the office. Nobody was talking to me. Kukaa tu for the whole day. When 5 o'clock reached I was expecting to be released to go home. Nikaambiwa hapana, you are going to sleep in a cell. Me I was very OK, I knew I was very innocent. No problem, I was very relaxed. Saa kumi na moja ilipofika wakasema twende. Singewaulilza kwanini wananipeleka kwa cell, Macharia na jamaa mwingine walinipeleka. Kunipeleka Kileleshwa, I stayed there for about 3 days.

It is when I landed in Nairobi High Court and they charged me with communicating information with unauthorized persons in contravention of the Official Secrets Act. They said until I hear from the A-G, we cannot give you bail. My family was in court but they did not know what was going on. Njoroge and Sisenda knew what was going on. I was denied bail till the A-G communicated to me and so I was taken to Industrial Area Remand. Nikakaa one week. Kukuja for mention after one week nikakubaliwa bond ya 200,000. Wakati my mother alisikia nimeshikwa ndio akapata shock. She was very shocked and could not believe it when she came to visit me in remand. Lakini, she could not believe. We talked for a very short time -- five minutes. Alikuwa amekasirika sana, she was very disturbed. Alikuwa ananiambia nimwambie vile nimefanya. Nikamwambia I'm very innocent.

So she thought I was lying and she was very much

annoyed. So ndio akapata stroke two days later na akapata depression. So she came to be admitted to hospital. Kwa sababu ya hii maneno tu. Before that she was healthy lakini vile alisikia nimeshikwa she got mad! Because she could not reconcile why I was arrested.

Are you getting me?

She said, Wamekushika, wamekushika! Watakuachilia? Umenfanya nini? When I was released after bond tayari alikuwa hospital so, naenda kotini, naenda kumwona. Alikaa hospitali karibu mwezi moja alafu she passed away. I was already on an interdiction and you just report at the security office and you leave.

Are you getting me?

Unareport alafu unanenda, unasign then you go on your way. I was being paid half salary. I had a case in court. After a month my mother passed away. It took a month for the A-G to say that there was no case against me.

My state of mind then was confused. Well, my family was supportive to some certain extent but it was not easy. Two months after mention the AG released me. I wrote a letter to CBK showing that I had been Nollé prosequi. They told me the bank no longer had confidence in me. After about a year I fled to Mombasa.

End of David's testimony.

David's brother, Daniel, also gives his and the Munyakei family's impressions of the trying time of David's arrest. Daniel is a master of understatement and though he describes his relationship with his late brother as cordial, he is the ideal bigger brother, someone who felt obligated enough to relieve their mother of paying David's school fees once he, Daniel, started working. This is in spite of the fact that their mother could still afford it and Daniel had only left school two years earlier.

It is characteristic for Daniel to simply say: 'I would treat him as a younger brother.' Sturdy, serious and organized, Daniel Munyakei's only frivolity is being an avid Manchester United fan.

This belies the logistical and emotional support he has provided David with over the years. All the more amazing when you learn that Daniel only got to know the real truth of his brother's involvement in the Goldenberg issue a few weeks before David testified in 2003. A weaker human being would have been swept away by insidious doubts and speculation.

Back in the 1990s, when a banker was thrown in jail it could only meant one thing - fraud. But even with that as a possibility after David's arrest, his brother Daniel fully supported him.

'Basically, my brother had pointed out that there was something fishy that was going on. I told him to be careful and try and find out what was going on,' Daniel says. 'But one thing about David you must realize is that he was a very courageous person. Basically he was born that way. He can easily reveal anything. Hii ni kitu imetoka utotoni. Brave. In school he was very open.' Daniel says that David was seriously disgruntled a year after being employed and often talked of seeking a departmental change.'

Eventually when he was relieved from Central Bank and put in, the word that was going around was that there was some confidential information that had been leaked from the Central Bank to the public through the MPs. We didn't even know my brother was involved - this was just something I overheard. Fununu za Nairobi. We did not connect the two.'

It took three days for Daniel to know that his brother had been 'put in.' Daniel says their mother knew almost immediately but she was so disturbed that she did not even tell him immediately: 'I tend to think that my mother got to know almost immediately. I could not ask why she did not tell me because I saw that that thing affected her very much. We did not want to dwell on that. We wanted to get him out.'

'Our mother did not accept that someone could just be wrongfully arrested and be accused of big things like that. More so her son. She could not believe that he could be involved. She initially thought that he had stolen. Open theft, forgery. Things like that. There was a heap of speculation.'

Daniel says that the fact that their mother worked in prisons and had seen men and women who were hardened criminals made it seem worse for her. 'She could not imagine her son one day becoming a prisoner. She changed immediately. After that she died on 10th July. Watu wakaanza kusema David amefanya mathee akufe because of criminal activities … '

'I went to see him in the Remand prison. He told me there was some confidential information that had been leaked and maybe that's why he was there. We left the matter there. It was very torturing. We did not involve any big figures to get him out because we did not know the core of the problem. It was a big surprise. This man has never been implicated in anything. And during those Moi times anything could happen. They were not allowing you to talk. Even when I went I could not speak to him alone. Those guys even interviewed me: 'You are his brother, where do you come from? Come and see him another day.' It was a big thing. We could see. There was a block between him and the public.'

'After our mother died, at the funeral we were imagining many things. I remember very well we buried our mother and then we travelled to be at the law courts on Monday.'

Another important cog in David's CBK years is the friend he had in the institution. In December 2004 David Munyakei met this friend, mentor and confidante Mr. Meshack Onyango Jamasai for lunch at the Nairobi Club. Mr. Jamasai, then a Deputy Director at the Central Bank, resembles a kindly uncle. With his large frame and small, warm, intelligent eyes behind round spectacles he looks like Eddie Murphy's character Professor Klump in 'The Nutty Professor.'

At the lunch, David Munyakei was very deferential towards Jamasai whose reaction to seeing his old friend was encapsulated in a question he posed to David: 'Munyakei, my friend let me ask you: How did you manage to do the thing that you managed to do?' That query shows the esteem in which both men hold each other even after all these years. Munyakei blinked several times and after trying to utter a few words was silent, almost shy. Nothing more needed to be said.

Part 4:
Transparency International, the Goldenberg Commission and How CBK and the Government Vomited on Munyakei's Shoes.

'They are my flowers. I enter my house and see these children .... These beautiful children that I cannot believe they are mine. When they run to me, shouting Dadee, dadee I know I'm blessed. Even on my way home, when I sleep in a nice hotel in Narok, I don't sleep as well as at home.'

David Munyakei talking of his daughters

ONE DAY IN 2003 David Sadera Munyakei got into a matatu and travelled to Nairobi to introduce himself to the Goldenberg Commission. His day had finally arrived. At the Goldenberg Commission offices, he met Mr Joseph Kamau, now the Head of CID. He introduced himself and talked for the next two hours to an entranced Mr Kamau, a career policeman who thought he had seen it all and might have told himself, 'This is one to save for my grandchildren.'

In our interview Munyakei said: 'Mr Kamau did not know who I was. I introduced myself. I was asked to bring all documents and all my particulars. I had buried all the documents in Mombasa and so I had to travel all the way and when I brought back the documents, these guys were shocked.'

'In April 1993 I had removed these documents from the Bank and smuggled them and hid them. I was carrying documents all the way to Mombasa.Immediately nikazificha kwa nyumba. I knew that one day that this thing must come out. I even have my CBK payslips. That is when they believed this is the man. I wanted to testify. They told me they'll arrange for me to testify and when I testified everything came out. You see, even my evidence was namba one.'

The rest is history. David Munyakei appeared in front of the Commission and sang. Things had finally come full circle. Flippant, petulant, direct and charming at the same time, David Munyakei finally became known to the Kenyan public.

The Kenyan media is the Kenyan media. They soft-focused Munyakei, and trained their lenses relentlessly on Pattni. Pattni became a cult hero. Munyakei was quickly forgotten. Kenya is all about size: the bottom line was that Pattni was a Big Man, and Munyakei was an ordinary Mwananchi. KTN could tell the difference.

In the words of one of the Goldenberg lawyer, Waweru Gatonye: 'If we had 10 witnesses like David Munyakei the commission could be closed in weeks. This is a man who is not coming to give us stories, he is coming here to give us tangible, credible evidence. He is not one of those people who come to waste our time.'

Munyakei was not oblivious of the effect he had on the Commission: 'My evidence was factual. Unajua ile kitu inaitwanga hands-on work experience. Siile kitu yakusema 'ilikuwa.' I had tangible evidence. Correct!' You know that thing called hands-on experience. Lawyer John Khaminwa even invited him for a cup of tea after his testimony. Munyakei had been drinking till 3 a.m the previous night, nervous about the next day's proceedings. Later, he would

confess: 'Nikipiga mbili ndio naweza kuongea.' When I
have two beers I find it very easy to talk.

David Munyakei's life changed after testifying and this
was the beginning of another Munyakei. In Olokurto,
the Goldenberg celebrity became a buyer of beers at
the trading centre. To avoid the crowds of thirsty locals,
Munyakei began drinking at the Olokurto police post
where he wouldn't be constantly hassled. Before he
testified, word all over the countryside was that Munyakei
had stolen from the Central Bank and in the ethical
framework of the Maasai nation he was to be despised
and drunkenly excororiated in bar corners. This did not
however mean that he was cast out - the Maasai nation
still recognized that Munyakei was one of their own.
And if any stranger came calling, they would protect him.
Like a disapproving parent the Maasai nation still loved
its prodigal sons. Now, after testifying, the truth came
out and Ole Shumbai was admired, respected and even
deferred to, in spite of his 'Otherness.' Ironically, this
meant that he would have to make forays into the world
that he had left when he sought sanctuary in the Maasai
nation. So one day while he was drinking at the Olokurto
police post, someone remarked about how even if he had
testified at the Goldenberg Commission he was still a
'maskini ya Olokurto,' an Olokurto poor man. Though it
is not clear what happened next, the police tried to arrest
David Munyakei but he made off, leaving his coat behind,
which he claims had Kshs 5,000 in it.

The next day the administrative police went to look for
him in what looks like an attempt to cow and arrest him.
Munyakei had already anticipated such an action and had
left early in the morning for Nairobi. Since he could not
board a matatu at the nearby Olokurto Trading Centre for
fear that the police would arrest him, he trekked 30kms

through shambas and backroutes to get to another nearby Trading Centre where he could board a matatu.

A few days later he appeared at the police post in a Land Rover full of askaris from Nairobi. All those who had taken this State witness to task got transferred after a few harsh words from above. From then Munyakei's stock rose in Olokurto. During the months after testifying at the Commision, a drunken Munyakei would often brag and even jokingly threaten to remove a gun and 'teach' those playing around with him a lesson.' Later, when Transparency International (TI) adopted him, TI was never far from his lips. It became TI this and TI that, all said in boastful exuberance.

At the same time, any media hype that may have swirled around David Sadera Munyakei soon dissipated. Having tried to expose the theft of billions of taxpayer shillings, and in so doing perhaps prevented the loss of billions more, David Munyakei once again assumed his hereditary place in Kenyan society – mind-numbing peasant obscurity. The media completely ignored him. Nobody from any of the dailies, or even the tabloids followed up to see how he was doing; whether all the lost years were being repaid.

Nobody checked to see what all those years in hiding had done to him. The Big Men hogged the limelight. The bright lights transformed Pattni from an arrogant little villain into a visionary martyr who had given his best years in trying to turn Kenya into "a mountain of gold". It would take another eight months for Munyakei to reappear on the radar of Kenyan consciousness, when he was nominated for the Integrity Award by Transparency International. A Big Institution had noticed him, so naturally the media noticed him.

In 2003 Transparency International started an initiative

called the Access to Information and Whistle-Blower Protection Program under their Advocacy and Coalition Building section, run by Jack Muriuki. The initiative was a program of activities meant to lead to the establishment of a whistleblower protection law in Kenya. Once a proposal was drawn up, the Advocacy team realised that they needed a face to complement their lobbying campaign. Enter Munyakei.

Transparency International, Kenya were also interested in David Munyakei as a nominee for the Integrity Award offered every year by Transparency International's Berlin head office. The Integrity Award winner is selected from a list of nominations forwarded by local TI chapters all over the world. It is a prestigious award. A few years ago, the slain Mozambican journalist, Carlos Albert Cardoso, received the award post-humously. When TI-Kenya was asked to forward local nominations, it came up with several names, including David Munyakei and Naftali Lagat. Both had played a role in trying to prevent Goldenberg from happening. Lagat had refused Kamlesh Pattni entry into the country with illegal stashes of gold.

One Monday in early September, TI Kenya had a meeting. Joyce Mwaniki, who was acting Head of Advocacy and Coalition Building in Muriuki's absence, told all present that they had a crisis on their hands; Munyakei needed to be found by the following Monday. A letter had been sent but TI was yet to receive a reply. TI-Kenya's assistant communications programme officer, Felgona Atieno, offered to find Munyakei.

Back then, Felgona resembled one of the female lead characters in Spike Lee's Mo Better Blues. She still has an air of innocence that fits perfectly with her frizzy hair, large eyes and tiny frame; nothing betrays the steel and resourcefulness within. During her four years at TI, she had built a list of high- and low-level contacts that would drop the jaw of an experienced Nairobi newspaperman. Felgona got on the case. In less than 48 hours she had made contact with Joseph Kimani, a Nation correspondent in Narok whom she had never met. He knew Munyakei and was willing to help TI trace him. Kimani advised Felgona: 'Please come with a 4 by 4 vehicle and leave Nairobi as early as possible.' Ignoring his advice, Felgona and TI driver Njuguna left Nairobi at 9 a.m on Friday and travelled to Olokurto in a van. This would prove crucial to their quest. They arrived at Olokurto in a swirl of suspicion. The trading centre clammed shut. They were strangers. Nobody would give them directions to Munyakei's home. Felgona looked around for a fellow outsider, somebody, something that was not obviously a part of the Maasai nation; she went to the police station. There she met officer Rono, who offered to show where Munyakei lived.

He wasn't home, and his children refused to answer any questions.

The sky promised rain. Rono advised them to get out of Olokurto immediately or they would be stuck there for the next two days at least. Felgona made a quick decision. They would go back to Narok and wait for Munyakei there. She gave Rono Ksh 250 for Munyakei's matatu fare. As they headed back, Rono spotted a woman in a buibui - Mariam, Munyakei's wife. They stopped the car, introduced themselves. Munyakei, she explained, had a fungal infection. He had gone to hospital. Felgona asked Mariam to request her husband to come to Narok the following day.

'Na sasa kama mna message ya Baba Naima si mnipe mimi ni mkewe.' If you have a message for Baba Naima please leave it with me, I'm his wife. Then the first drops of rain fell. Felgona, Njuguna and Joseph Kimani hurriedly got into the car and drove off. Having ignored Kimani's advice – "Come with a 4 by 4" - they slipped and slid and almost overturned. In Narok, a bucket of rain is enough to turn the black cotton soil roads into chewing gum.

The next day Kimani didn't show up on time. He had described Munyakei to them ('You know when the white settlers were here, eh? Munyakei has that blood. He is a Masaai but he is very light. He looks like a mzungu.') but what good was that? Even if Munyakei did show up would he speak to them without Kimani, somebody he knew, being there? A man fitting Munyakei's description walked in. Felgona went up to him and introduced herself. He mumbled something, deeply suspicious and barely concealing it. Then, as Felgona fidgeted, Kimani walked in. But it did little to loosen up Munyakei.

A clumsy three-way conversation began, Kimani acting as go-between, translating a strange code full of mutters for Felgona. No, he hadn't received a letter. The odds that the letter would reach him were like him winning the charity sweepstake. He hadn't been to town in months, because he didn't have the money. The address belonged to a friend he hadn't seen for an even longer period of time.

Suddenly inspired, Felgona offered them a drink. Munyakei began to relax after the second beer. Felgona explained that TI wanted him to come to Nairobi to give his consent for the nomination for the Integrity Award. She told him about the whistle-blower program, about how it was possible that Parliament would soon make it law precisely because of how Munyakei and others like him had suffered for speaking the truth, how it was important to protect truth-sayers, whistle-blowers.

Munyakei was definitely listening now. TI-Kenya had

nominated him because they thought that what he had done was very important, crucial, that few people had displayed his courage, and that now there was a good chance that he would be acknowledged on the world stage. Would he come to Nairobi and sign the forms? He asked when. She told him and gave him transport money. He gave her a phone number, that of the only booth in Olokurto near Mama Jane's shop. That's where he could be reached.

Suspicion had been replaced by tentative trust. On Monday he was in Nairobi at TI offices near 'Community' signing the nomination forms, and everybody in the office was walking around in amazement, wondering how Felgona did it.

David Sadera Munyakei's resurrection happened through a series of trips between Olokurto and 'Community.' TI-Kenya arranged for the treatment of his fungal infection. A few weeks later, he was declared joint winner of the Integrity Award, along with Corporal Lagat. The trips became more frequent as preparations for the award ceremony, which would coincide with TI-Kenya hosting in Nairobi, for the first time, the 10th anniversary of the Transparency International movement.

Munyakei would star in two promotional videos, one commissioned from Berlin specifically for the Integrity Awards and the other commissioned by TI-Kenya. Director Judy Kibinge was commissioned to shoot the second video and she travelled to Olokurto with her film crew in October. Though it was Jack Muriuki whose Advocacy section was interested in Munyakei as the human face of Whistle-Blower Protection Program, Advocacy never really got to know him. It was Felgona who ended up being his minder by default. Inadvertently playing mother hen, she held his hand, listened to his every wish. Advocacy kept him at arm's length; Felgona coddled him.

Felgona says that many people in TI felt that she had become too close to Munyakei. There were times she was left out of the loop. Once, TI sent an investigator to interview Munyakei in Olokurto and since they did not want him forewarned, Felgona was not informed. One day just before the Integrity Awards, she received an unexpected call from Munyakei asking her why she hadn't told him that TI had sent a man to come and interview him. She told him she did not know what he was talking about. It ended up being a comical affair. In Olokurto, Munyakei began to get impatient when the investigator didn't show at the agreed-on time. So he went to the trading centre to kill time, ended up in a bar, started drinking and forgot all about the investigator, who had arrived two hours late and was now sitting at Munyakei's house making small talk and waiting for Baba Naima to return, msubiri alienda hapa tu, atarudi hivi karibuni.

Eventually at about five pm, Mariam, suspecting her husband's whereabouts, went to fetch him, and dragged him back home, he grumbling: "Huyu mtu anataka nini, what does this man want? Asisumbue maisha yangu, he shouldn't stress me," and Mariam beside herself that Baba Naima ataropoka, would implode embarrassingly in front of the stranger at home.

In the end, David, with customary skill, managed to pull himself together and the two got along like a house on fire. False alarm, needless anxiety: it turned out that the man was not really interested in character issues but rather in ascertaining whether Munyakei was living in poverty, the true test of integrity. The investigator left at dawn, after a night-long bonding session and a good time had by all.

Munyakei relied on Felgona for everything. Arriving at the office and not finding her, he would refuse all offers of food and drink. 'Singekula mpaka hukuje,' he would say. Mariam would jokingly refer to Felgona as mke mwenza, my co-wife. Such relationships of dependency can be found in all whistleblower accounts. The Oscar nominated movie 'The Insider' is a case in point, and it dramatizes how tobacco industry whistle blower Jeff Wigand, played by Russell Crowe, rocked America with his revelations. The movie also depicts the close relationship between Al Pacino's character, a TV producer from the show '60 minutes' and Russell Crowe's whistleblower.

TI received a wide range of public responses after David Munyakei's story came out in public through the promotional video, a radio programme broadcast by TI and the Integrity Awards. After the Integrity Awards, whistleblowers started crawling out of the woodwork. The radio programme was flooded with calls.

Transparency International single-handedly pushed Munyakei's case. No other anti-corruption organization or civil society body has ever really been interested in David Munyakei. TI wrote on several occasions to Central Bank Governor Andrew Mullei enquiring on the possibility of his reinstatement. CBK remained silent on the issue. Informally, CBK had said that it plans to set up a legal committee to look into the case of David Munyakei. A source at the CBK revealed that his name once came up at a board meeting but was shrugged aside when a powerful individual said that Munyakei had broken the rules and there was no case for his reinstatement.

Even after a change in regimes, there was no sign that the Office of the President had seen fit to intervene on his behalf. The government of Kenya has yet to award him for his services, even posthumously. On Jamhuri Day 2003, Lucy Kibaki led the list of who's who, honoured for bravery and integrity and service to the nation by President Kibaki. Ordinary Kenyans were, as usual ignored. Munyakei's treatment by the government strengthens the suspicion that most Kenyans harbour - that the Kibaki government has served only to benefit the little coterie around him, the Makerere Boys, the Muthaiga Golf Club Gikuyu, the Mt Kenya Mafia.

In January 2004 TI contracted the legal services of Nderitu and Partners, Advocates, Public Notaries and Commissioners of Oaths to press the reinstatement case. The lawyers wrote a letter to the Central Bank Governor, Andrew Mullei. He never responded.

```
***
Nderitu & Partners Advocates, Notaries
Public & Commissioners for Oaths
W.N. Nderitu Ll.B. (Hons), Dip. Law
A.T. Njoroge Ll.B. (Hons), Dip. Law
Your Ref: Our Ref: N&P/MISC
Date: 10/1/2005
Governor,
Central Bank of Kenya,

P. O. Box 6000,NAIROBI
For the personal attention of
Dr. Andrew Mullei


Dear Sir,
```

DEMAND FOR THE REINSTATEMENT OF DAVID SADERA OLE MUNYAKEI (PERSONNEL NO. 2400)
We are writing to you under instructions from our client, Mr. David Sadera Ole Munyakei, a former employee of the Central Bank of Kenya, whose services were terminated

due to "unsatisfactory conduct" with effect
from 21st September 1993.

Our instructions are (and, we believe,
that it is now public knowledge that) Mr.
Munyakei's services with the bank were
terminated as a result of information he gave
to the Hon. Professor. Anyang' Nyong'o and
the Hon. Paul Muite in April 1993 relating
to illegal and irregular discounting of
CD3 forms in favour of Exchange Bank and
Goldenberg International through Central
Bank preshipment finance scheme. As a direct
consequence of Mr. Munyakei's actions, the
paying of fictitious foreign exchange claims
was brought to the fore, and this eventually
resulted in a mitigation of the fraudulent
loss of public funds. We are instructed that
Mr. Munyakei's actions, which were done
in good faith and in the best interest of
the Central Bank in particular and of the
country in general ought not to have called
for the termination of his employment. In
particular, Mr. Munyakei's actions were done
with a view to ensuring maintenance of a
sound monetary system and ensuring compliance
with international agreements to which Kenya
was a party, in accordance with the Central
Bank Act, Chapter 491 of the Laws of Kenya.
Indeed, the job offer to Mr. Munyakei dated
4th January 2005 by the Government of Kenya
(copy enclosed) is proof that the Government
does not consider Mr. Munyakei's conduct to
have been "unsatisfactory" as alleged in the
letter of dismissal.

You are no doubt aware that criminal
charges brought against Mr. Munyakei for
alleged breach of the Official Secrets
Act, Chapter 187 of the Laws of Kenya, were
eventually terminated.

Our client therefore finds no basis
whatsoever for his dismissal in the first
place, and the refusal to reinstate him to

the service of the Central Bank despite
request. Our client further contends that the
appellate procedure that was supposed to look
into his plea for reinstatement was a sham,
as he was not given any opportunity to defend
himself either prior or subsequent to his
dismissal.

   Please quote our reference when replying
   V.A.T. Reg. No.: 0108921Z PIN: A002298809Z
    Accordingly, we are instructed to demand
that you admit liability for the wrongful
termination of Mr. Munyakei from the service
of the Central Bank of Kenya and for the
payment of compensation arising due to
the wrongful termination. We are further
instructed to demand that you undertake to
unconditionally reinstate him to service,
after which the issue of the quantum of
compensation payable will be addressed.
   TAKE NOTICE that if you, (as the chief
executive officer of the Central Bank and
the office under the Central Bank of Kenya
Act responsible for the Bank's management,
including the organization, appointment and
dismissal of staff) do not admit liability
as aforesaid and reinstate Mr. Munyakei to
service within thirty (30) days of the date
of service of this letter upon you, we are
instructed to file suit against you.

   Yours faithfully,
   For: Nderitu & Partners,Advocates,
   WILFRED NDERITU
   Cc: David Sadera Ole Munyakei
   /lawn

In January 2004 the government offered David
Munyakei an accounts clerk position at the Office of the
President. At Kshs 8000 per month, his salary would be
slightly more than half his monthly pay at the CBK in

1991. By the end of 2004 the CBK owed David Munyakei Kshs 2m in back pay – this is a conservative figure that does not take into consideration annual salary increments and promotions. Though his life had already been tragic, it became a veritable comedy of errors when the numerous visitors he had since achieving hero status came calling – after calling Mama Jane's phone booth to announce their imminent arrival. An interview by some Standard reporters ended in such drunken riotousness, it seemed a miracle that they were able to put together an in-depth Munyakei story later. And there was always the danger, of course, of taking a joke too far, or not getting it, or maybe even realising that the joke is on you. Like the time the elders from the nearby community arrived with a special request. It was soon after the Integrity Awards, which had been presented on the same day that Wangari

Maathai won her Nobel Prize. 'Some of the elders appeared on my doorstep. 'Tumesikia Wangari Mathaai ameshinda award na amepewa pesa. Tumekuja kuuliza: What Are You Planning? Labda yako haikutangazwa kwa sababu ya security – naimekuwa ni pesa mingi kushinda za Mathaai." A funny note crept into Munyakei's voice as he recounted one incident: 'Walikuwa wanatarajia mbuzi. It was hard to convince them that the award did not have any money.' We heard that Wangari Mathaai has won an award and been given money. We also know you won an award and we wanted to know what you are planning. We understand that your cash award has not been announced because of security because it is more than Mathaai's. They had expected me to at least slaughter a goat. Munyakei said: 'Since that day I told my wife to keep the award away as it will not solve my problems.'

Part 5:
A Schizophrenic Interlude, The Suit

'Its like when I tell people I'm a Maasai - and they say no. I've learned you don't have to tell people anything about what you are. Wanakataa. Wanasema how comes. Hata Mombasa I didn't have to tell them anything. No? They said I was a mbarawa, they did not know any Maasais.'

(David Munyakei)

IN FEBRUARY 2006, the police arrested a young lady named 'Shamsa' who was actually John Kamau, an 18-year old man. 'Shamsa' had taken to dressing as a Muslim woman some time before. He had been employed in a BuruBuru household as a housemaid for a year before being discovered. His real identity was only un-covered when he tried to convince neighbouring teenage daughters that they could make money prostituting themselves to men he knew. The girls' parents found out, 'Shamsa' was arrested and John Kamau was exposed.

In explanation, Kamau said he dressed as Shamsa because of 'shida' – he needed to survive. The story of David Munyakei, otherwise known, to the Kenyan public as the Goldenberg whistleblower, lends itself to the Shamsa saga. 10 years ago, David Munyakei, half Masaai, quarter Kikuyu and quarter white, 'disappeared' into Mombasa and became a Muslim, leaving behind the going-ons of that little shop of horrors we now call Goldenberg. He became an inconvenient hero, yes, but also a shape-shifter of extraordinary ability, all to avoid 'mkono mrefu wa serikali'. For that he is a study in Kenyan self-exile. Before he passed on, to negotiate his celebrity status he would summon up those abilities.

During KBC radio broadcasts David Munyakei would slip into a Maasai Swahili of such guttural authenticity that his own wife would hardly recognize him. Mariam, who only discovered the true origins of her husband after they were married for a year, now realized that her husband was a shape shifter and talked of how this role-playing extended even to their visits to her parents in Lamu: 'Mama na baba hawaamini ni Mtoka bara, hawajawahi kumsikia akizungumza lugha yake. Hata sasa akiwa yeye hubadilisha Kiswahili chake kabisa hata huwezi jua ni yeye. Mwanzo akiwa kwa baba huwa mungwana sana kwa mzee. Ile hata ukamwambia mzee eti Baba Naima hunywa anaweza kakupiga kofi 'niondokee waniambia mambo ya upuzi!' Atakuona wewe mrongo sana. Babangu ni mtu wa dini sana. (Munyakei) anakuwa mnyenyekevu sana, hata ile sala 'Allahu Akhbar' Baba Naima ndiye wa kwanza kumwambia babangu 'saa zimefika, twende msikitini.'

Huyo huyo ndiye mume wangu na ndiye Mola alinipa. Unajikaza tu. Unasema huyu ndiye aliyenipa mwenyezi Mungu, na huwezi kukwepa. Nikutu unachosikia kina kuburuta kama ngombe. Kwetu unajikaza.' You cannot convince my parents that David comes from came from inland. Even today, his Swahili changes completely when he is talking to them. Especially when he is with my dad, he becomes very polite and well mannered. If you were to tell my dad that (David) drinks he would slap you. When he and my dad are together (David) is the first to invoke Islamic greetings and remind my father that time to go to the mosque has come. His Swahili would change completely when he was talking to them. Especially when he was with my dad he would become very polite and well-mannered. If you told my dad that David drinks he would slap you. But that is the husband God gave me and I had to stay with him. You have to be strong.

Even his less voluble brother, Daniel Munyakei, recognized that David knew how to talk to people and 'go about things.'

Fast forward to December 2004 a time when Munyakei seemed to be living in a curiously schizophrenic but altogether very tight space. He would board a rickety Hilux in Olokurto at five am after waking up at three. There were only two vehicles every day and none during the rainy season till the rivers of mud revert to rivers of dust. He couldn't afford to miss any of these cars. He would change vehicles in Narok, and alight at Nairobi's 'Nyamakima' carrying nothing but a toothbrush in his pocket. He would be wearing faded old-school jeans, cheap white plastic sneakers and a checkered threadbare flannel jacket, and always a sweater inside, no matter how hot it was in those days just before Christmas of 2004.

At times his skin would appear unhealthily congested. The spots on his cheeks from his fungal infection were still evident. His first stop would be Transparency International and there they, who had been receiving him for months, might have started to feel how draining altruism can be; Christmas was around the corner and they had families to think of. They wanted to close shop early and get on with the festivities.

Munyakei was work, part of their jobs. Many felt he could wait till January. During this period Munyakei would walk into Transparency International (TI) and, depending on who he was preparing to meet, quickly change into the suit he testified in back in September before the Goldenberg Commission - The Suit, which now was permanently parked at the TI offices. Navy blue, sky blue shirt and tie sprinkled with what looked like herons. On wearing it, David Munyakei would be transformed. You suddenly saw the ex-CBK man. Now a hero, The Suit was useful for meeting, say, Onyango Jamasai for lunch at the Nairobi Club. On his way in, he would bump into Hon. Anyang' Nyong'o – to whom, together with Hon. Paul Muite, Munyakei had smuggled the evidence that eventually broke Goldenberg wide open. When they bumped into each other, Hon. Nyong'o, then Planning Minister, somewhat curiously asked Munyakei what the government was doing about his case.

Or The Suit could be for a Nation Media Group interview. One Friday afternoon a clueless Nation reporter walked into Transparency International and as soon as he began to interview Munyakei, it became clear that he had not done his homework. The questions he was asking had already been responded to and published in the newspaper he worked for. Munyakei smoothly turned interrogator, and adviser, giving the hapless reporter an unused angle for the story – telling him to focus on what happened at Safari Park at the Integrity Awards ceremony.

'Kiraitu Murungi instructed me to report back to work in front of many, including John Githongo,' Munyakei told the reporter. 'And up to now I don't have a job. That is the story.'

The Suit could be for meeting lawyer Gibson Kamau Kuria, now a friend. It could be for those with whom David Munyakei could share his views on the Narc government, the economy and, of course, Goldenberg. He would excoriate the Kanu regime and hint at his own political ambitions come 2007. Everyone loved him, and The Suit was a perfect fit for the part. Then it would be time again for David to go back to Olokurto and The Suit would come off at TI.

One time before leaving for Olokurto, he visited his old Mombasa friend, Peter Kariuki and stayed the night. Kariuki was shocked at David's physical appearance – he remembered David as being much heavier and more light-skinned - but even more shocked that the old David whom he had known as a well-groomed young man could wear the same shirt for three days. In Kariuki's house David had a strange dream, of having a conversation with fellow Integrity Award winner Naftali Lagat. The men had many similarities. Lagat, who has been lucky enough to retain his job, had also been arrested by the CID after he refused to let Pattni bring smuggled gold into the country. Like Munyakei, his integrity was intact; he had been offered a Ksh 2m bribe and he had refused.

After the visit to Kariuki, Munyakei carried a large box of Christmas presents on his way back to Olokurto. As the matatu got onto the highway, he wondered idly whether the ram he had spent a whole day looking for before his journey to Nairobi had been found.

Enter Munyakei the Olokurto farmer. The wayward ram in question had begun to stray since he started lending it to the neighbours to impregnate their ewes. At one point during his search for the senge, he had come across a herdsman he knew who was wearing a yellow cap emblazoned 'Ngombe,' a barbed wire brand, that seemed to suggest a permanent solution to Munyakei's senge problems.

Down the hillside was a stream and lovely grassy meadow. For years the local chapter of the African Inland Church (AIC) had baptized children like a young David Munyakei there. The man hailed David from afar: 'Sadera, sopa!' Greetings.

'Sopa oleng,' replied Munyakei, his eyes scouring the countryside for a glimpse of fleece in the shrubbery. He came within arm's length of the herdsman, leaned on a fence, Maasai style – one hand holding the fence and his right foot placed against his left leg in a triangle.

'Natafuta ndume wangu. Dunia ni mbaya. Wale vijana unajua sasa hakuna pesa-labda hao vijana wameuza hiyo senge,' David said bitterly. Greetings. I'm looking for my ram. Things are bad-I'm sure some kids have stolen it as it's January and there is no money. The herdsman remained quiet.

'Afadhali ningeuza yeye nilipoona kisirani yake. Afadhali. 5000 ingenisaidia sana. Nipate kitu ya kula Nairobi.' I wish I'd sold that damn ram before he became difficult, always looking for females. Now I would have 5000 kshs in my pocket to eat when I go to Nairobi.

'Sadera,' the man now offered, 'hiko vitu mbili. Ukate makende ya huyo senge ama umuuze.' Two things. When a ram reaches a certain age you either castrate him or sell him-otherwise your life becomes very difficult.

'Eeeeh. That is true,' Munyakei laughed. 'Ama.' The man continued, 'nilikuwa na ndume kama hiyo na siku ile aliipata kisirani nilimkata makende. Hiyo kazi ikaaisha.' Sadera laughed in appreciation. That's what I did with mine-once people started to borrow him to climb their ewes he started becoming crazy and I cut off his balls.

'Sema aki, sema aki,' he said. Hear Hear. There was a green combine harvester in the distance and the two turned to look as its teeth threshed the ground before it. Suddenly the sky released a few large drops and David shrugged himself out of his reverie. In the distance towards Olenguruone where the rain was easing up, rays of sun burst through the clouds, God's Hand reaching down to earth. It was a scene straight out of those children's pictorial Bibles. Munyakei was oblivious to the splendour. He returned without finding his ram, a poorer man.

His daughters were as pleased as always to see him and jumped about him as he walked in and sat in his favourite seat. His youngest, Sally, pulled at his beard and Naima and Fatma bullied him into listening as they read from the animal chart on the wall in high piping voices.

'Peacock ni Tausi!'

'Elephant ni Ndovu!'

'Lion ni Simba!'

'Drums, drums, drums!'

'Dadee Tiger ni nini ...'

All along their father gazed at them like a man awoken from a dream. In his face comprehension finally stirred. These three little angels belonged to him. And as the sun set and night came, their voices carried far into the silent, starless sky.

Part 6:
The Final Chapter - Let Us Now Praise
A Hero, Long Day's Journey Into Night:
The 9 O' Clock News

'Every hero becomes a bore at last.'

Ralph Waldo Emerson, US essayist & poet (1803 - 1882)

Heroing is one of the shortest-lived professions there is.

Warren G. Harding, former U.S President (1865 - 1923), Speech in Boston, 1920

TWO YEARS LATER around 9 p.m in the middle of July 2006, I received a call from a colleague and friend, investigative journalist, Parselelo Kantai. I was in an editorial retreat, away from Nairobi, near Isinya, past Kiserian, a place not unlike Narok where I had spent 4 months of my life with David Sadera Munyakei, the Goldenberg whistle-blower, who had receded into a swirl of memories. Isinya was like Narok, both in demeanour and temperament, with its low sky, sweeping wind and nights that came down upon you in seconds. The founding editor of Kwani?, Binyavanga Wainaina, and I were working on the upcoming 4th issue of the magazine. We were on 18-hour watch, chugging at full steam and on Day 2 of production, at that stage when it becomes difficult to distinguish times during the day and hours during the night. We did not need any distractions.

'Hey, have you heard ...' Parselelo was calling from Nairobi. There was background pub clamour.

'Are you at Sippers?' There was a pause on the line and I watched a huge moth chase lamp shadows in my room - a room coloured in soft bedspread browns, towel-oranges and cream walls and ceiling.

'No I haven't heard,' I said. I expected another major NARC blooper from the new NARC government of small farcical crises. 'Have you heard' automatically brought on dread inter-mixed with whimsical expectation. In the space of several months, First Lady Lucy Kibaki had stormed the Nation Media Group offices in her pajamas, government-sent commandos had ransacked the offices of the East African Standard and trashed the newsroom's computers, Armenian mercenaries had invaded Kenyatta Avenue, and MPs in their tens 'visited' a collapsed two-storey building on Ronald Ngala Street while half the country starved. Around that time the State offered the panacea of prayer to cure all our ills as Kenyans, urging us to get on to our knees for a whole working day and pray for succour. 'Have you heard' could be anything.

The moth kept doing its noisy rounds. I remember this little detail perfectly. Death always seems to take me back to where I was when the news came. So I would remember the moth, a harbinger of death in some cultures. I would also remember that part of me felt safe and insulated. Nairobi, with its petty concerns and Ringling Brothers circus act – a stage where the political clowns rule and the soapie, Cuando Seas Mia, plays on prime time television every Saturday night. It becomes a faraway, intense, and bizarre world when one is in the plains of the Rift Valley on assignment.

Parselelo's voice came back over the line: 'Munyakei

passed on two days ago. Nobody knows what happened. Will find out more and call you back.' He clicked off as I scrambled with questions. I went outside into the dark low night. Out there and with this new information, the prefab cabins now cast a cheap ominous shadow against the low sky, no longer safe from anything at all. I looked into the plains and could not distinguish their grey-blue tinge cast by a small moon from that of the Kajiado night sky, low, heavy and ponderous with the false promise of rain, stretching out for kilometres. It was as if I had been given a canvas and the times I had spent with Munyakei flashed in an instant on that plain. I deliberately willed snapshots of him, trying to hear him laugh, talk in his guttural half whisper; something I had learnt to do since childhood in similar times of tragedy when death came calling. Flashback: The night of July 2005, the night David Sadera Munyakei received the Firimbi Award, one of the last full instances we were to spend several hours together. And as I remembered that under that Kajiado sky-plain, oblivious to the large moths in all their entropy fluttering over me, the tears failed to come. I sighed and went to give Binyavanga the news.

A few days later I watched sound bites on KTN and Nation TV - Goldenberg Hero Dies -four minutes of classic doublespeak on each channel, blandly told. Through my jaundiced eye I scoffed at what seemed like a struggle to construct a narrative capsule of heroism from David Munyakei's life. I watched the continuity announcer fail in 'advert' tones to capture the text and essence of this Everyman hero and plant it in the Kenyan psyche. When I remembered how Munyakei had lived destitute, friendless, unprotected by the country he helped save; as I watched the babble of static incoherence, the freakish tribute many years too late, hard knots of anger overcame and I started shouting at the bland continuity. But in a flash it became immediately clear to me that this was the only possible label you could go out with in Kenya; when you were a Hero, you had to be a Loser. A look at the quasi official list of heroes that had been proclaimed for the last 40 years was delightful testimony to this – an ongoing narrative of the Kenyan Hero-Loser. Like the English poet Auden once said, no hero is mortal till he dies. Munyakei in death had once again become human and we wrung our hands because we had done nothing for him. I started planning my trip to Narok to pay my last respects.

It was at least one and a half years since I had properly seen Munyakei. The only image that stayed with me was the man surrounded by his little girls after he had come home without finding his senge, the ram. Though we had stayed in touch, our relationship after the first part of the story in Kwani? 03 had been published had become one of rushed phone calls, quick cups of coffee. It was mostly my fault – I was caught up in my search for the next Big Story and partly living in the Rift Valley over the first six months of 2006.

One of the last times we had spent any meaningful time together was at the Kenyan Human Rights Awards. I remembered watching him receive the Firimbi Award and on failing to get the ear of either the First Lady, Lucy Kibaki, or Uncle Moody (the Vice President then, Hon. Moody Awori) the whole evening, he finally got a palm rub by both on their way out. Munyakei came back to our table full of exuberance, happier than I had seen him in those last few months. He hefted his award - the Firimbi Award an impressive wire sculpture offered to public heroes by the Kenyan Human Rights Commission - onto the table.

'Uliniona nikisalimia Lucy, First Lady?' You saw me

greet Lucy, the First Lady? I nodded. We went out to Choices, a popular pub in the concrete Industrial Area for drinks. There was a sad but festive air between us. This was at the end of four long months of being together. I am not sure that he was as simultaneously relieved and sad as I was that it was all coming to an end. For him, his one act of bravery and self-lessness would never go away. He would have to live it for the rest of his life. As it were, Kwani Trust was about to publish his story in its 3rd issue. I would be just one of the clowns who had to finally leave the stage.

As I thought about all this, he brought up the subject of money – he needed some. After all I had become a friend and we could talk about it. I gave him the usual spiel, bringing up the NGO/CBO he wanted to launch for the millionth time and he went quiet. After that we mouthed inanities, tried to attract some females to our table in between long and companionable silences interspersed with long sips of our Tuskers. After another girl turned up her nose at us, Munyakei would try and convince me to take him to Modern Green.

At some very late hour, I idly turned to him and, with the prescient insight of total intoxication, detected something in his form and face that I hadn't caught before. It could have been the slight skew to the prop of his shoulders, the way the club lights fell on his point-five (half-cast) lightness, the slight hunch of neck and upper back; it could have been the third sip of a flat beer but at that moment I sensed something- a whiff of illness. It came and went in a flash and an overwhelming sadness caught me. To fend it off, I rushed to the loo, stuck my finger down my throat and let it all out. The bad vibes passed.

When I came out into the corridor, another lanky girl

of the night who I'd observed dancing all night not far from our table, was standing there in a T-shirt and tight jeans. Expecting her to ignore another of my overtures like many had done that night, I mumbled a Hi. She looked closely and curiously at me, into my red swollen eyes and sighed: 'Don't worry. Be happy.' And gave me her number. We hugged and I went back to Munyakei. 'Nilikuwa nadhani umeniwacha,' he said. I thought you had left me.

Morning came and the bar closed. Munyakei and I went outside into a bright new day. The sun had just come up – the world was light blue with an infrequent burst of yellow from the sun's rays. It was going to be a hot day. I could feel a headache coming on. I put Munyakei into a cab and paid and told the driver to take him to his hotel. Part of me was aware of the futility of the request. With the sun rushing at me I watched him, eyes slitted, trying to keep my feet, drive away to Modern Green. I turned away with sudden tears in my eyes. There had been much laughter that evening. But I could not help but feel that that bright new day was an end to something.

The next time I saw Munyakei was at the launch of Kwani? 03 at Carnivore. Just like at the Integrity Awards years before, he seemed like a deer caught in the lights. We hardly exchanged more than several sentences that night. I spoke more to his wife, Mariam, who was as exuberant as ever. Munyakei seemed preoccupied and faraway. He responded to my queries on the NGO/CBO he was planning to start with monosyllabic grunts.

After that meeting and the launch of Kwani? 03 and Munyakei's story, there was an overwhelming reception of the story in the journal that translated into a keen interest by the mainstream newspapers. Before long the East African Standard had agreed to serialise four parts of the full story. Just after the second part of the series had run I received a phone call from Munyakei – he sounded frantic and asked to urgently meet me. Getting a lift from a friend I picked him up at G.P.O. on an overcast Tuesday morning. As we drove away and I looked up at the high-rise windows of Nyayo House, Munyakei casually mentioned he had just come from there.

'Sema Haki! Siku Hizi Una Gari,' he sighed. I see you are driving nowadays.

'How are you …' For some reason I couldn't tear my eyes away from Nyayo House.

'Central Bank wamenipigia simu asking what I'm doing. They've called me.'

'Who called you…?' I felt some paranoia creep in – we cleared Nyayo House – Former House of Kenyan Pain and Biting Reality – and got on to the Uhuru Highway roundabout.

'They asked me how I think I expect to get my money when I'm going to the newspapers like this …'

'We published your story months ago. Why now?'

'Kwani? si gazeti …kila mtu anasoma gazeti' Kwani? is not a newspaper.

Everybody reads newspapers.

'The people I talked to say they are trying to organize my money and I should be patient. They told me the newspapers are not going to help me …'

'The Standard plan to run two more articles …' I said.

'Ai. Apana Standard wawache hiyo maneno…' No. Tell the Standard to stop… He did not mention he had already gone to their offices and raised up a stink.

'Let's go meet Binyavanga and talk about it,' I said.

I immediately called Binyavanga and explained everything. Binyavanga told me the Standard had already called him wondering what was going on. We decided to meet immediately to sort out this fresh crisis on our hands. As our voices carried over the empty airwaves I knew it was going to be one of those long Nairobi days by the end of which you have a dull throbbing headache after spending thousands on airtime. The sky was still overcast but the day was building into a scorcher. Everyone, everywhere was sweating up their windscreens. It hadn't started raining but there were traffic jams and hooting everywhere.

Maybe Kibaki is on the road, I thought idly, and thanked God I wasn't hungover. Munyakei smelled of beer but looked oblivious to the oppressive atmosphere.

'Nitafutie kama hiyo,' he said pointing at my phone when I was done with Binyavanga. Get me one like that one.

'Let's go meet Binyavanga. Tuongee hii maneno.' So we can talk about the matter.

'Wapi?'

'Westlands.'

'Ehh. Sasa mko Westlands. Kama ningejua ningeshuka hapo nikitoka Narok. Billy umenitupa.' You've moved to Westlands. If I'd known I would have dropped off there from Narok. You've really forgotten me, Billy.

'You know Nairobi. It's madness. A month is like a fucking day,' I said.

'Haya. Twende ununue lunch.' Okay, let's go, you buy us lunch.

'Binyavanga yuko aje…?' How is Binyavanga…?

'Yuko sawa.' He's O.K.

'Lakini hiyo maneno ya Standard muache,' he said

casually, oblivious to newsroom pressures and operations. Yes. Leave that Standard stuff alone.

Uhuru Highway sped by. Munyakei suddenly laughed from the back seat. I turned to him and he looked at me shaking his head.

'Wewe Billy ...' he laughed. 'Umenona ... maisha mzuri.' You Billy you. I can see that you've grown fat. Life looks good. We all laughed, a deep-from-the-belly-laughter, all the way to the eyes. For a moment there was no Standard newspaper, there was no unfairness and the world was a bright place full of promise and hope. And for the first time since I'd picked him up it seemed like the good old times in Olokurto where we had spent so much time together.

'Wapi mbuzi yangu?' I asked him. Where is my goat?

'Eeeh. Wacha tuone Binyavanga na alafu wakubwa wengine. Serious. Alafu tuongee hiyo maneno. Senge utapata.' Let us to talk to Binyavanga then some Big Men. Then we can talk about your ram. My friend who was driving turned to me sotto voce.

'Hey, I thought senge means faggot. Whasup?'

I looked at the miles of car ahead of us on Uhuru highway. Mid-morning traffic. 'Take some time and get out of Nairobi. Senge is a male goat, sheep, whatever. I guess the gay anology comes from the satyr which has a goats head. Read up on your fucking Greeks,' I said.

'Greeks? Not me. Too gay. And ... ' He gave me a long look. 'Be nice. I'm chauffering you around.' I reached for the radio, going off mid-morning, Queen of Babi-lon City, Caroline Mutoko and twiddling the dial till I found Nonini, Nairobi's poet of pander, whim and sexual innuendo.

'Man, I wish it was a Friday,' I said to no one in particular.

'What are you doing turning off Kenya's Oprah.'

I settled back into my seat.

'Nimetoka mbali, Nimetoka mbali,' Nonini sang. 'Nimefika bila Busu FM mia moja.'

As we crawled along Uhuru highway I could not help turning back from my shotgun seat now and then to look at Munyakei. The Standard matter had gone away and I decided to let it rest till we met Binyavanga. Turning towards Munyakei for the fiftieth time I couldn't help but think how there is always something hit and miss about trying to get to know someone who is already a public personality; someone who the lights have hit full on the face; someone who has had their five minutes of fame; someone who is known of by more people than he knows. People like this seem to have a jumpy essence– hard to pin down, always shifting as if they are playing for an invisible camera, having a million conversations in their heads, eyes not really focused on you but playing to a whole crowd of souls behind you.

That was the Munyakei in the back seat. For him, fame came from being in court before the Goldenberg Commission, from being in a large hotel hall before a panel of international journalists, from having conversations with corruption and human rights bigwigs and being recognised by Government Ministers. And with it came a certainty of his place in the world.

I momentarily let the Standard matter rest because I saw a million cogs and wheels turning behind that face, now a veneer of forced busy-ness, that I had come to know so well, the eyes full of a million angles. Noting my perusal he blurted out, suddenly and oddly: 'By the way I can't stay. What is all this about? I have many people to see. Watu wa TI. Felgona. Mzungu mwingine alinipigia simu.' People at TI. Felgona. Some white man who has been calling me.

'Relax,' I said.

We got to Westlands and there was Binyavanga and Wambui Mwangi, a Toronto based professor of Political Science, sitting and waiting for us at Café Lambada. Professor Mwangi, who also had an essay published in kwani? 03, had been sufficiently moved by Munyakei's story and was trying to set up a fund for his children's school fees. Munyakei and Wambui had been working together for the last few weeks. Munyakei ordered tea: 'Nataka kama ile ya nyumbani. Si maziwa separate, maji separate, sukari separate. Wacha iboil mpaka imwagike naifanye cchhhh.' Make for me tea the traditional way. I don't want any containers, sugar separate, milk separate, water separate. And let it boil till it goes ccchhhh.

He turned to us. 'There has been problems in communication between us. Even before the problem of serialisation came in I had been trying to get in touch. I am not saying you did a bad job with my story. There are small things, there are small corrections but we have been overtaken by events. When I went to the Standard I was saying, I was telling the Standard people that if this story is running it is better for us to meet so that I can edit the story. And then make a few amendments and then continue further serialisation and even now they are very much ready. They said they would preserve space to run the story and they are waiting for all of us to call them.' He paused looking around for the waitress. There was some kind of piano music playing in the background and it lulled as all to his narrative.

'Where is this young girl?' Munyakei asked. 'Yes. I never edited the story. After it appeared in the Standard I was called by some guys in the CBK and they were not amused by some certain issues. CBK as an institution are not amused. I admit for now that things have been overtaken by events. The Standard story has made a big impact. And it is generally something like that that I wanted to talk to you about and that's why I called Billy. Many of them, the CBK people haven't read the whole book. They don't go to the bookshop but when they heard it is in the newspaper they rushed to see.' His voice dipped and bobbed with the piano music, every word an intonation to every key – time seemed to stand still around the table.

The waitress appeared at the table and we stirred. Munyakei looked up. 'Nipe samosa mbili. Na si ya mboga. Mi ni Maasai. Ya nyama. Ama Billy? But I am also a Kikuyu like you,' he said laughing. Two samosas, and not vegetable ones. Meat samosas. I am a Maasai. Yes Billy?

'There is no problem. I am saying all this is subject to discussion.' We all sat there listening to our own thoughts. He played to his new crowd.

'You remember when we met the first time, you know my problem. You remember you said utaenda uaangalie vile unaweza kunisaidia. Sasa when we came for the launch we actually expected that you will give us something. You see. Sadly that was not the case; we had hoped you would give us something. I am not saying that it is a must. Because there was nowhere we had written – this was just a mutual agreement. Nashindwa vile nitasema. What can I say.'

The self-doubt in his eyes from back in the car became more evident. And that essence that had seemed so elusive in the car, like a ping pong ball on speed, became like warm heavy millet porridge. He had three faces: doubt, entitlement, and hustle. That day I would see them all. At moments they would become interchangeable. I suspect that doubt had become ascendant over the many weeks I hadn't seen him. Maybe now as he finished addressing us he was thinking that he should have demanded some things earlier that would have helped avoid scenarios like the one we were now in. Maybe he thought he should have just added something after his excellent Goldenberg testimony that had stopped the whole nation in its tracks, turned to Goldenberg Commission chairman, Bosire and Co. and simply asked for help: 'I would like to add something if my Lords shall allow me … I am poor. I am destitute. Please help me.'

Maybe he was thinking that he should have ducked under the wooden pulpit reaching below his waist and, like his antithesis Pattni had done, said: 'a mosquito has bitten me my Lords,' making the whole nation laugh. After all, most Kenyans, having learnt their law from Vioja Mahakamani, the local court-based comedy, expected some humour. Maybe, as he sat with us at Café Lambada that day, he was thinking that he should have added something after his speech at the Integrity Awards: 'I am very grateful for this Glass Award but I have no bus fare to go home.' The doubt in his face was of the kind that dawns on one upon realizing that they are at some kind of crossroads, when the gears fail to click together and the equation fails in the shaken test tube. Munyakei blinked and some of the certainty returned, he hadn't forgotten how to be Kenyan and schizophrenic.

It was agreed that Munyakei and I would go over to the Standard to reassure them that everything was okay and that they could continue with the serialisation. As we drove back into town, the issue of money came up. By that point it had been agreed that any profits from the serialisation of the story were to be written out as cheques for Munyakei's daughter's fees. It now seemed that he had changed his mind somewhere between Westlands and the I&M building, worried that everyone was leading him on a merry dance.

Right at the ground floor of the I&M building, having been cleared to enter the offices of the Standard but waiting for someone to come down and seen us in, Munyakei suddenly turned to me: 'Can I get some of the money now?'

'Standard pays at the middle of the next month after the appearance of any story ...' I said with dread.

'Wanalipa nani? Who gets paid?

'The writer gets paid.'

He grinned. 'Wewe?' You?

The receptionist looked at both of us. 'Please move to the side.'

'I have pledged in public that I will give half of the proceeds for your daughters education,' I said.

'Ai. No cash now. No story now.' He looked at the clock on the wall.

'Lazima niende Chester House kuona mtu,' he said suddenly. I have an appointment at Chester House. And just like that he walked off. Moments later, the daily editor of the Standard appeared – ready to usher us upstairs. He smiled on seeing me alone with my crestfallen face. There was no need for words. We shook hands and he went back up.

It was 2 p.m, August, 2005. After that day, I would see David Munyakei only twice before his death. As I went outside the sun seemed brighter than ever – July was over and its chills were behind us. The Standard called off the serialisation. They refused to proceed without Daid Munyakei's overt assent.

At that moment it occurred to me that very few people would believe the exchange that had just taken place. I do not know why I thought it unbelievable, but really it was just another deal gone wrong in a contemporary Kenya that was all about the hustle. The Kenyan of 1992 and the Kenyan of 2005 were two different entities. So it was with Munyakei. As I stood there I remembered a story a friend once told me about his travels to Narok back in 1992 and how you could take a thousand pictures in Maasailand and people would actually smile and wave at you. Today, if you were to take the photo of an 8-year old girl, she would come up to you: 'Nataka unilipe. Kwa nini unachukua picha yangu?' I want you to pay me. Why are you taking a photo of me? In those 13 years Kenyans had started listening to the smallest violin in the world, the kind that plays the mbeca tune between fore-finger and thumb. Munyakei, I had just learnt, was no different. Part of me, like many who encountered him as the Goldenberg hero, expected him to be the same, and had freeze-framed him circa 1992 – as the Goldenberg Hero.

Everyone in Kenya was in a hustle of one sort or another. What I, as a writer, called a pitch to the Editor was just a hustle of sorts. And everyone around me was hustling and calling it something different. And what Munyakei had been trying to do since I met him that morning was just his way of hustling.Was that so bad? Maybe a hero wasn't allowed to hustle. In part, the Kenyan preoccupation with getting paid had been rushed into being by Goldenberg itself. By almost destroying the Kenyan economy, Goldenberg had ushered in the age of the Kenyan hustle. And just like Kenya, Munyakei had also changed. He had adapted.

As I stood there looking at the multi-storeyed, startlingly blue I&M building, institutional headquarters of the Standard and KTN, a place where I would come to pick up a cheque I also realised that what had happened was understandable. Munyakei had probably stopped understanding the language of institutions after being betrayed again and again over the years by the same. Why would he listen when I told him of an institutional requirement where cheques were picked up after two weeks? CBK had after all been promising to do something for him for years.

I thought back to the conversation in Westlands and realised that it had happened at cross-purposes. We, as institutionalised individuals, were speaking to the 2005 version of Munyakei as though it were the 1992 model hero who sat before us. Maybe he had never been helped all these years because he had been having what he saw as the same meaningless cross-purposes conversation all along. While many said they wanted to help him, he simply wanted to get paid. When everyone said they were just doing their job, all he saw was that they were getting something and he wasn't. And that had started on that day in 1992 when he shouted, Eureka! I know where these billions are going. Look. Look. Look.

But then again he had forgotten that many of those trying to help him could and would still get paid without him – by being 'Kenyan' and trying to make himself a product for sale, creating his own hustle, he had removed any chance of being 'helped;' because the very reason he was being helped was because he was imagined as somebody outside such an earthly transaction as the hustle. Many of his 'helpers' worked for institutions that frowned on the hustle. So very few of his helpers, myself included, wanted to have that hustle conversation. His self-appointed helpers thought it was not their job to have that conversation. We were all caught up in a brilliant Catch-22 scenario – and the problem was that everybody was living in absolutes, on either side of the hustle. His helpers wanted a hero and he wanted a few thousand shillings. So eventually Munyakei went his way and the helpers went theirs, which meant Kenyans out there would not read his inspirational story in the mainstream press. I went outside I&M and called it a day.

Though I hardly saw David Munyakei after that, many of those who he had been in touch with at Transparency International say he continued to come into Nairobi between late 2005 and early 2006. By the time Kwani? had published his story in mid-2005, he had already moved his family from Olo Kurto to Narok, mostly for convenience and for the sake of his children's education.

Munyakei continued to keep in touch with Felgona Atieno, his handler and self-chosen confidant at TI since he won the Integrity Award. Even when she left TI for a brief stint he continued calling her. For him it was all about human contact, not what he had come to see as institutional massages through meaningless awards. By March 2006, he had taken up the clerk's job at the Office of the President, earning a net salary of Kshs 8000 a month. He was clearly a desperate man and before he took up this job he had kept talking up all manner of schemes to anyone who would listen.

At times he would say he had come up with a contact who would be sending him to Dubai to bring stuff to sell. Other times it would be ideas on leasing a farm and planting wheat. Maybe the most viable of all these schemes was a Trust Fund he was trying to set up with Kituo Cha Sheria, and a scholarship application to the U.S. At the time of his death he had been placed on a waiting list for the latter.

During the leaner times he was not above regretting what he had done, blowing the whistle. Felgona says he was full of doubt. 'He constantly regretted doing what he had done. He constantly regretted not agreeing to the bribe by a senior governmental official to go to Uganda and start a new life,' she says. Many other times he wondered out aloud why organisations like TI, KHRC and Kwani? could not give him money. In truth, the world had moved on. TI had a new administration and the new kids on the block not only didn't know him but would never have had any idea how to handle him. Kwani Trust had moved on to another publishing cycle and was busy working on their fourth book. The new NARC Government had started feeling and looking so much like the previous one, it felt as if they had been around just as long. It was a new brave world and Munyakei 2005 was not part of it because everyone wanted him to belong to the past.

So he wisely took up employment with the Office of the President, living with a relative at Nairobi Dam estate. He later had to move to Kawangware when the former rented the place out. Life was tough over those few months but somehow he managed to go to work and visit his family every other week. He also applied for a transfer to Narok and was waiting for a response from the O.P. when he contracted a gum infection. An infection that was serious enough to warrant his new employer to let him off till he recovered. Munyakei travelled to Narok towards the end of June 2006 to recuperate. He would never go back to work again.

On July 30th 2006, 6.30 p.m David Sadera Munyakei would pass on peacefully at the Narok District Hospital.

The True Story of David Munyakei

Part 7:
Back Into The Future

SEVERAL DAYS AFTER I heard the news at Isinya through Parselelo Kantai, I travelled to Narok to retrace Munyakei's last days. I had already missed the funeral which, following Muslim law, had happened just 5 days after Munyakei's death. He was buried on a Friday. I travelled two weeks later back into a town I had spent quite a bit of the first part of 2006 in. As usual it was unfamiliar as hell. The initiated will tell you Narok town is pure perspective and perception, like its hinterland, Narok district. Any definition of Narok, like most places of unlimited access, is based on what you make of it. As a town and district it is relative to how wide you open your eyes, your wallet and your mouth.

Since its neighbours are the highly populated districts

of Kiambu, Nakuru and Kericho, eyes are always swiveling across its porous borders on 'unused' large tracts of land and moving in and out. 'Everyone thinks land here is for the taking,' a provincial administration official once told me. And with the steady erosion of the Nairobi-Nakuru road and the building of the new tarmac road between Narok and Kisii, and hence Kericho, Western Kenya and Kisumu, traffic has increased. When you talk to locals they are bemused by the cultural yoke, and the perceived 'backwardness' that visitors have imagined upon them. And yet the town is the district headquarters of Narok District, the second largest district in Kenya bordered by Nakuru, Kericho and Kiambu. To all eyes looking in, there is the perception of kilometers and kilometers of unused land. And when waves of land-seekers stream into the district they come to Narok town.

The physical reality of Narok town is like that of many smaller Kenyan towns outside Nairobi and like them has little urban planning but has loads of informal money. To the unjaundiced eye Narok is a dusty sprawl full of low rise, metal-balcony faced structures with signs proclaiming: 'We deal in both roughware and software' and 'A business with no sign is no business.' Unlike other Kenyan towns, acacia trees thrive under petrol stations, dusty and smoky-grey from the spewing of fuel from trucks. It is built in a large hollow dip and when it rains on higher ground, Narok can flood even as every roof remains dry.

Getting to Narok town can be a major farce. Before getting into town on one of the worst roads in Kenya, one reads a huge sign: 'this road has been repaired by Petroleum Levy Funds.' The road in places looks like the tar that has been gnawed away by a giant rat with vehicles having to take to the flattened roadside tracks. After the never-ending death ride the throat tickles and the coughing starts. There are myriad road blocks, always manned by five different institutional representatives: Kenya Police, Narok County Council Administrative Police, KWS Rangers, Administrative Police and Government Foresters. All share the takings from charcoal bribes, timber trailers, illegal squatters harvesting from the forest and who knows what else.

Narok is a very liquid town with money from Maasai Mara which is controlled by the Narok County Council (the richest county council in the land), the leasing of land for the growing of wheat and barley plus extra coming from Maasai livestock. The collection of the newest taxis one will see outside a Nairobi Jatco fleet sitting before a street full of mean tempered structures is testament to this. The taxis are so new and clean they seem immune to the dust, a mirage. Still, there are reassuring generalities on the street. Maasai males in shukas lean on long staffs watching the world go by from sidewalks, tourists with peeling skin oppressed by sun and dust peer from the windows of speeding Land Cruisers heading to the Mara. The odd tractor chugs by, spewing grey exhaust into the azure sky as wide as God's eye. Traditional Maasai women sit by colourful wares on the streets and young men fill the streets, most of them land-brokers.

At night, Narok is both a truck town and a town built of trucks. The low-rise structures fade into the background. Dust becomes a cloak of darkness. Greetings of 'Sopa Oleng' change to the proverbial 'Sasa.' Every street fills with trucks. The town becomes one huge truck made up of these mechanical insects coming in all sizes. There are small lorries with religious scripts on their behinds and huge Transami trailers guarded by up to five guards. Canters with incongruous loads take to pavements covered in dirty tarpaulins. That is the exterior of Narok town at night.

The town's inner night soul is the bars and small discos with 70's names like Hillside and Equator, that can be found all over trading center and small-town Kenya, Karatina to Nanyuki. Aside from the road of good intentions, there are four major roads that cut through large flat swathes of the Rift Valley into Narok town and they bring with them all those who understand that Narok is the perfect meeting place of 'easy' money and little aesthetic. Girls from Meru, Kisumu, Mombasa and Kisii flock to Narok during 'harvesting' season in the months of May to September. Fat hardened women with brown teeth and red eyes peer at you from chicken-fence grills behind bars with bottles titled Tornado and Senator.

There is a saying in Narok: 'Kuingia ni rahisi, Kutoka ni balaa.' Entering is easy. Leaving is hard. Narok has an accepting culture, and there is money here. This is where Munyakei moved his wife and three daughters in 2005, away from Olo Kurto. They came to live with Munyakei's aunt Emily, his mother's sister in an area called Mungare. Most of the non-Maasai people in Narok, largely Kikuyus and Kisiis, live here and in adjoining areas called London and Mungare. If one were blindfolded and taken into any one of these areas at night and the blindfold removed they would immediately think they were in Dandora.

Enterprise goes on till late in the night between the small stalls, kiosks and structures, and it is hard to differentiate housing and commerce, shelter and subsistence. Movement of man, woman, child, goat, dog, cow and chicken goes on from morning till late. Small butcheries, video parlours showing premier league games, vinyozis, mitumba stalls, small electronic shops build the narrow streets of these living areas in Narok. However, unlike most of their counterparts elsewhere in Kenya, Mungare and its neighbours are relatively safe. The Munyakei family moved into a small plot with five single rooms belonging to his Aunt Emily. The family were given two rooms. This was in April 2005.

The following is a transcript from his wife Mariam Sadera, nee Mariam Ali Muhammad Hani, describing David Munyakei's journey from sickness to death.

My husband came home towards the end of June, 2006. His face and teeth were so swollen that he could not eat anything solid. There was nothing we could do but wait for his salary so that he could buy medicine for his gums. We just bought medicine from the shops.

We even forgot about his phone and it went off and no one from work could even get hold of him. Then one day when he was about to travel to Nairobi to get his salary and treatment he suddenly became better. He travelled to Nairobi for his salary and there he was told that his transfer had come through and his salary sent to Narok.

When he came back to Narok he was informed that his salary had waited for him but had been sent back. At this time he had been planning to travel to Nairobi to attend the Saitoti hearings on July 31st, which was the following week, and he became saddened. Our daughters Fatma and Salma were also chased away from school. David became so quiet that we all became worried.

He stopped eating and talking and seemed to get

pneumonia and after a few days we decided to take him to Tenduet hospital. He was breathing heavily and seemingly in such heavy pain that we had no otherwise. But we could not afford it and instead took him to Narok District Hospital, which was close by, on Saturday, July 30th, 2006.

We got there at 1 p.m and could not afford to pay for anything. The doctor agreed for him to stay there as long as we could pay for drip and food. We were asked to give him milk and medicine recommended by the doctor. At the time he could only be fed through a teaspoon which I did everyday.

On Sunday we went to see him with a change of clothes but the doctor asked us to leave him. We were asked to give him milk. The doctor kept on asking how serious his smoking had been. On that Sunday he seemed fine and his face had regained colour. For the first time in days he seemed to recognise me and when we went in he made a gesture for me to remove the buibui from my face. I removed it but when he tried to speak nothing came out of his mouth. So I gave him milk and medicine and left sure that he was going to recover. I had to travel to Ewaso Nyiro at 2 p.m to go and pick up some money from another aunt for his drip. I got back at 7 p.m.

When I asked Auntie she said that everything was okay but when I looked inside the house I noticed that the bottles of drip we had bought earlier were there. So I asked what was happening – later I would learn he had already passed on but everyone was trying to find a way to break the news gently to me. Eventually I was told. My husband died at 6.30 p.m that Sunday.

Epilogue

Now we will know who the true revolutionary is ...
Zimbabwe, Bob Marley and the Wailers

AFTER INTERVIEWING Mariam Munyakei I headed back to Nairobi and the T.V sound bites I had watched in Isinya came back to me in a series of flashes. As I remembered the boob tube's flickering on in sonorous tones constructing a Hero, I thought of Dedan Kimathi, General Mathenge, that generic Mau Mau freedom fighter figure, individuals like Bildad Kaggia. I remembered watching Munyakei being served up, Hero a la carte, Kenyan style, on T.V, and came up with a check-list of the factors that qualified him as bonafide Kenyan Hero.

Firstly and obviously, like many before him he was dead. Secondly, he had done the no-man's land act of heroism, suspending himself perfectly in obscurity between that one heroic act and death. Thirdly, his name had occupied an uneasy place in the Kenyan psyche, a kind of token admiration intermixed with a cynical dismissal. Fourthly, he had received some recognition from either the media, the NGO community or a foreign country and become a Koigi, beloved of the Norwegians, a Ngugi wa Thiongo who was considered a revolutionary in Southern Africa and more exalted in Uganda and Tanzania than in Kenya even during his long-awaited homecoming in 2004. Fifthly, Munyakei had not 'officially' betrayed an interest in earthly rewards; and sixthly, like all those American superheroes he had a villainous alter-ego who went on to reap his just desserts. Like every Batman he had his Joker. Like every Dedan Kimathi, he had a golden-eyed figure who had dazzled the masses. Like every Mau Mau freedom fighter, he had a home guard pulling a miraculous photo finish at the Uhuru ticker tape to become ascendant in the new Kenya. He was a General Mathenge for whom there were innumerable collaborator - chiefs' sons who had become our new rulers. And he was a Bildad Kaggia living in Jericho for whom there was a horse riding, crop carrying David Mungai or a villager king like Kariuki Chotara. For Munyakei there was Pattni. But to be texted, to enter the written historical record of Kenya and in this to fulfil the seventh criterion and the most significant one of them all, Munyakei joined Kenya's pantheon of heroes by falling off the radar of the State. He became the Hero who had died a Loser. He had come full circle: from Zero to Hero and back.

On T.V:

'Munyakei was born on 21st June 1968. He passed away two days ago after a short illness.'

Next clip: 'Honorable George Saitoti appeared in the High Court for a hearing of his role in Goldenberg...'

Munyakei's life and all that had happened to him goes up there as one of the biggest farces this country has seen in its national life. Many officials were acquitted of their alleged roles in the Goldenberg scandal. This was after Munyakei had sought re-employment to the CBK for no less than 14 years. The Goldenberg commission collectively took home millions of shillings. Weeks before, the Munyakei family had struggled to raise Kshs 350 for a bottle of drip, a few hundred shillings for his girls to go back to class, funds for the funeral.

That is Kenya. I remembered visiting his unmarked grave in the Narok muslim cemetery and going to his old watering hole, a bar named 'Memories.' Millions of memories flooded me suddenly through that journey back to Nairobi, and as we drove through the Rift Valley night the tears again came. The famous German playwright Bertolt Brecht had once said: 'Unhappy the land that needs heroes.' He should have added schizophrenic and corrupt is that land that ignores them and exults them in death as losers.

During the Goldenberg Commission, Munyakei testified that 'My lords, I think by exposing the irregularities, I was doing a great favour to this nation.' His story seemed at first to lend itself to the easy cliché of David and Goliath. Later I discovered this was a complex narrative with many twists and turns.

In spite of all this one thing remains clear, and that is that David Sadera Munyakei suffered ignobly for his efforts to right something he saw as wrong. All the players, good and bad, in the Goldenberg fiasco landed squarely upon their feet. Meshack Onyango Jamasai, one of the good guys, who alerted him to what was going on, was last a Deputy Director at CBK. Hon MP Anyang' Nyong'o subsequently became the Minister for National Planning and Governance before becoming a leading opposition

123

figure. Paul Muite held on to his post as MP until finally being voted out in 2007. Kamlesh Pattni has become a cult hero through the (mis)representation of our media - Saul became Paul. All the players who have been accused in one degree or the other still enjoyed the largesse of Pattni years after the scandal broke. Other individuals such as Mr Sisenda, Munyakei's immediate superior and the head of Department Mr Njoroge, Goldenberg's Tweedledee and Tweedledum, remain free men and did not even appear before Goldenberg to explain their roles in the matter.

When David Sadera Munyakei was in the darkest of moods he felt that he had become a victim of his own making. And in such moments he bitterly said: 'There is no use suffering for the larger good. If this were to happen again I would not do what I did.' The young naïve man who joined CBK eventually lost a lot of his innocence. He became a 'Kenyan.' Contrary to what he might believe, David Munyakei is a Kenyan tragedy, a victim of our times and ways.

His role in stopping the processing of false export compensation claims and hence halting the systematic looting of taxpayer's money at the Central Bank cannot be gainsaid. David Munyakei helped save the Kenyan economy from collapse and perhaps ushered a new Kenyan day by exposing what will always remain a dark period in this country's history. And for his efforts all David Sadera Munyakei ever received was a a dark blue suit from Transparency International and a glass award.

The following astute observation has been made to explain acts of whistleblowing: 'Many are sincere and correct in their assertions, having become whistleblowers reluctantly after failing to change their organization through more mainstream or acceptable channels. Some